PETITE KITCHEN

MY
FAMILY
TABLE

MY FAMILY TABLE

SIMPLE WHOLEFOOD RECIPES FROM 'PETITE KITCHEN'

Eleanor Ozich

contents

introduction

My family and I started on our journey to simple and wholesome eating a little over three years ago, after our little girl, Izabella, developed a troublesome skin condition that doctors and specialists couldn't treat, and after also noticing a decline in our own health and wellbeing. It was during this time that I started writing a daily food blog, which I named 'Petite Kitchen'. Each and every day, I would share recipes and ideas from our new way of living.

It became beautifully obvious to me that whole, natural foods can be a wonderful form of medicine that can help heal, cleanse and renew body and mind. This wholesome way of living has helped our little girl, Izabella, in a way I cannot even explain — and the positive impact it has had on my husband, our son Obi, and of course myself, is just incredible.

Sharing recipes: it is simply what I do, spending hours in my kitchen perfecting dishes and trying out new combinations. I am hopelessly addicted. Nothing makes me happier than being able to pass on my new ideas and inspiration to others.

Within the pages of this book, I hope you will experience these beautiful moments spent in my kitchen. I have poured my heart and soul into compiling a selection of simple, wholesome and delicious recipes designed for the whole family to enjoy. These recipes are centred on the idea that food is to be made with love and care, and to be eaten together, around the family table.

I strongly believe in buying good-quality produce, free-range eggs and sustainably farmed meats wherever possible. I understand this kind of produce can be a little more costly, but I also believe that each and every time you buy good-quality food, you are investing in not only your own, but your family's, health and future.

Take Mother Nature as your guide, and cook using seasonal fruit and vegetables. Not only is this a beautiful way to embrace nature's fruits, it is also far more cost effective, delicious, and a wonderful way to help support the community around you.

With a few exceptions, most recipes in this book are naturally gluten-free, or I have included options to make them so. I love using different and exciting types of flours and grains. These alternatives taste fantastic, and quite often offer more nutrients. I have also included a lovely range of vegan, vegetarian and dairy-free options too.

I prefer not to make anything too fancy or extravagant — just real, everyday food, prepared simply, and absolutely packed full of flavour and deliciousness.

So join me, from my kitchen to yours, as we celebrate wholesome food in all its glory. Roll up your sleeves, dog-ear the pages, spill ingredients and, in turn, transform my simple recipes into your own proud creations. Eat, enjoy and, most of all, share this wonderful way of living with your family and friends.

Eleanor Ozich

raising children on a wholefoods diet

Both my daughter, Izabella, and son, Obi, are very curious about and interested in food. The first thing they ask when they wake up in the morning is, 'What's for breakfast, mama?' They absolutely love trying out new and exciting flavours.

I have to admit, however, that raising our children to eat wholesome and healthy food has not always been easy — it takes a lot of hard work, commitment and dedication, but the results are well worth the love and effort. Every child deserves to understand where their food comes from, and how it helps them to feel good and to be full of energy and happiness.

I believe that taste and a love for food develop in early childhood, and that our children will grow to like most of the foods we offer them. It's never too late to introduce wholesome food to their diets, although this is a little easier if done earlier on.

Here are a few tips that may be helpful for you and your family.

◆ Kids want to know about food; all you have to do is start a conversation! Talk about where it has come from, and how it will benefit them by giving them more energy. Get chatting about your favourite flavours, colours and textures of food.

◆ Try to make healthy choices, right from the beginning. Children are far more likely to grow up loving the foods they are used to eating early on, although it is never too late to introduce healthy foods. Make one small and simple change per day, and in no time you will begin to notice positive results.

◆ Be consistent with your approach. When I offer something to my kids that they are not so keen on trying, I give it a little time, and then try again. Consistency is the key to building good and strong habits.

◆ Lead by example. By eating a well-balanced and varied diet, children are more likely to be interested in trying out what you are eating.

◆ If your child does not want to eat something, do not punish them or make an issue of it, as this may form negative ideas around food. Instead, I find that ignoring protests and staying calm helps them realise that they are not going to get any rewards by acting out. Continue to enjoy your meal at the table, and do not drop what you are doing to make them something alternative to eat. Quite often their hungry tummies get the better of them, and they in turn start to enjoy what you offered them in the first place!

◆ Have healthy and wholesome snacks on hand for when you are out and about, and for school lunchboxes. This can help avoid the temptation to buy processed or fast food. I have included a chapter here called 'On the go', which is packed full of healthy snack ideas, but you'll also find plenty of other recipes in this book that can also be made into snack-size versions.

◆ Let the kids get busy in the kitchen. Children love to participate in cooking, whether making their own lunches, helping out with baking, or even washing fruit before eating. They are more likely to try something new and have a higher appreciation for something they have made themselves.

◆ Last, but not least, make the family table a place where you all sit down as often as you can, and enjoy the pleasure of food together. The family table is the best place to build beautiful and happy memories around food.

The recipes are coded as follows:

GF ◆ GLUTEN-FREE
DF ◆ DAIRY-FREE
VEG ◆ SUITABLE FOR VEGETARIANS
V ◆ SUITABLE FOR VEGANS

A
NOURISHING
START
TO THE DAY

*I believe that in order to embrace the day
wholeheartedly, we must nourish our bodies
with a wholesome breakfast.*

I grew up in a household where the first meal of the day was
mandatory, so unsurprisingly I have continued this morning
ritual with my own family — whether that's enjoying a warm
slice of toasted rustic walnut bread with butter, simple baked
eggs with tomato, spinach and mozzarella, a quick round
of creamy smoothies before heading out the door, or going
all-out on the weekends and making the most delicious sweet
almond crepes with ricotta and honey grilled stone fruit.

We all need different types of breakfasts on different days,
so I have included a wide range of recipes in this chapter
to help you feel inspired.

Enjoy.

rustic sesame honey bread

*Bound with free-range eggs, this rustic loaf is delicious toasted
and topped with the gorgeous combination of avocado, tomato and basil.
It keeps really well in the pantry for up to a week.*

MAKES 1 LOAF ◆ GF, DF, VEG

For the bread
200 g (7 oz/2 cups) almond meal
60 g (2¼ oz/⅓ cup) tapioca flour
   or potato flour, or 40 g (1½ oz/
   ⅓ cup) cornflour (cornstarch)
3 large free-range eggs
2 tablespoons honey, or maple
   or rice malt syrup
80 ml (2½ fl oz/⅓ cup) olive oil
60 ml (2 fl oz/¼ cup)
   coconut cream
1 teaspoon bicarbonate of soda
   (baking soda)
1 tablespoon apple cider vinegar
a pinch of sea salt

For the topping
3 tablespoons sesame seeds

Preheat the oven to 160°C (315°F). Find a loaf (bar) tin that is about
12 cm (4½ inches) wide, 23 cm (9 inches) long, and 7 cm (2¾ inches) deep.
Line it with baking paper.

Combine all the bread ingredients in a large mixing bowl and mix until
well combined. Spoon the batter into the loaf tin, then even it out with
the back of a spoon. Sprinkle the sesame seeds over.

Bake on the middle rack of your oven for 45 minutes, or until a skewer
inserted into the centre of the loaf comes out clean.

Remove from the oven and turn out of the tin. Place on a wire rack and
leave to cool completely before slicing.

The bread will last for up to 1 week in an airtight container. It also freezes
really well; for added convenience, cut it into slices before freezing.

soft-boiled eggs with poppy seed parmesan toasts

A perfectly simple breakfast of soft-boiled eggs with golden, crunchy parmesan soldiers. This dish, for me, brings back lovely memories of learning how to crack into eggs while sitting at my grandparents' breakfast bar. This recipe is dedicated to my beautiful Grandma Alza and Grandad Norman. I love you both more than I can say.

SERVES 4 ◆ GF (using GF bread), VEG

8 free-range eggs, at room
    temperature
8 thick slices of rustic bread
60 ml (2 fl oz/¼ cup) extra virgin
    olive oil
a large handful of grated
    parmesan cheese
1 tablespoon poppy seeds
butter, to serve (optional)

Preheat the grill (broiler) to 180°C (350°F). Line a baking tray with baking paper.

Bring a medium-sized saucepan of water to the boil. Turn the heat down to a gentle simmer, then carefully lower the eggs into the water, using a slotted spoon. Boil for 1 minute, then remove from the heat, cover with a lid and leave the eggs in the water for about 4–5 minutes.

While the eggs are cooking, slice the bread lengthways into fingers, or 'soldiers'. Using a pastry brush, spread the olive oil over the slices, then place on the baking tray. Sprinkle the parmesan and poppy seeds over the top. Grill (broil) the fingers for 3–4 minutes, or until nicely toasted. Remove from the oven and leave to cool for a minute or so.

To serve, place four egg cups on four separate plates, along with a teaspoon and a dollop of butter, if using. Crack open the tops of the eggs, then serve immediately, along with the crispy toast fingers.

a nourishing start to the day

banana oat hot cakes

*My whole family are crazy about these hot cakes, which rarely make it past
the stovetop onto the table. My daughter, son and husband literally stand right
by the stove, watching over my shoulder as I flip the hot cakes in the pan. As soon
as they have cooled just enough to handle, they are quickly devoured. You could
serve these hot cakes topped with some lemon curd, plain yoghurt, whipped cream,
or home-made plum and orange juice compote (see page 80). They'll be a true
family favourite for years to come, I am sure.*

MAKES ABOUT 20 ◆ GF (using GF oats), DF, VEG

2 large bananas, roughly chopped
4 free-range eggs
50 g (1¾ oz/½ cup) organic rolled
(porridge) oats

Add all the ingredients to a blender and whiz until smooth.

Lightly grease a large frying pan over medium–low heat.

For each hot cake, ladle 1 large tablespoon of batter into the pan;
you should have room to cook three pancakes at a time.

As soon as little bubbles start to appear, turn the hot cakes over,
then cook for a further minute or so on the other side, until golden.

Serve warm, with your choice of toppings.

baked eggs with tomato, spinach & mozzarella

One gorgeous morning, not wanting to spend too much time indoors, I whipped up this simple skillet breakfast for the family. After 10 minutes in the oven, it went straight into some bowls and was devoured in minutes, outside in the garden, sitting barefoot in the green grass, enjoying the beauty of nature.

SERVES 4 ◆ GF, VEG

3 large handfuls of baby English spinach
60 ml (2 fl oz/¼ cup) extra virgin olive oil
2 tablespoons balsamic vinegar
2 large heirloom tomatoes, roughly chopped
125 g (4½ oz) buffalo mozzarella, sliced
8 free-range eggs

Preheat the oven to 220°C (425°F).

Combine the spinach, olive oil and vinegar in a bowl. Toss well to coat.

Transfer the spinach mixture to a large ovenproof frying pan and top with the tomatoes and mozzarella. Carefully crack the eggs in and around, then season with sea salt and freshly ground black pepper.

Transfer to the oven and bake for 8–10 minutes, or until the eggs are cooked to your liking.

Carefully remove from the oven, divide among plates and serve.

delicate
chamomile
muffins

◇◇◇◇◇◇◇◇◇

recipe page 24

LOW
BUSH **BLUE**
PRODUCE O

delicate chamomile muffins

These muffins are lovely as a light breakfast, and have a beautiful fluffy texture.
I have added plenty of lemon zest to the batter, which imparts a bewitching perfume
as they bake in the oven. These muffins are also perfect for kids' lunches,
or as a quick and wholesome snack on the go.

MAKES 10 ◆ GF, DF (using coconut cream), VEG

185 ml (6 fl oz/¾ cup) coconut
  cream, or 185 g (6½ oz/¾ cup)
  plain yoghurt
3 free-range eggs
125 g (4½ oz/½ cup) coconut oil
90 g (3¼ oz/¼ cup) honey
160 g (5½ oz/1 cup) rice flour
100 g (3½ oz/1 cup) almond meal
2 tea bags of dried chamomile
  leaves (about 2 tablespoons)
zest and juice of 1 lemon
1 teaspoon bicarbonate of soda
  (baking soda)
1 tablespoon apple cider vinegar

Preheat the oven to 160°C (315°F). Grease 10 holes of a standard
muffin tin, or line with paper cases.

Add the coconut cream, eggs and coconut oil to a food processor.
Blend until smooth. Add the remaining ingredients, then pulse until
well combined.

Divide the batter among the muffin holes. Bake for 20–25 minutes,
or until a skewer inserted into the middle of a muffin comes out clean.

The muffins will keep for 2–3 days in an airtight container, and can be
frozen for up to 2 months.

Recipe photograph on page 22

the perfect green smoothie

Below are some simple tips for creating brilliantly creamy and refreshing green smoothies for the whole family. In the warmer months, I quite often make a round of smoothies for the four of us as an afternoon pick-me-up. They are wonderful when you are feeling in need of a little boost of nourishment.

I like to keep my smoothies basic and not too complicated. For example, in the smoothie pictured on page 27, I have added ½ avocado, 1 small frozen banana, 250 ml (9 fl oz/1 cup) coconut water, a large handful of cos (romaine) lettuce leaves, the juice of ½ lemon and a small handful of fresh green grapes to a blender. Just whiz until smooth and enjoy.

Here are four simple steps to creating your own delicious green smoothie.

◆ To begin with, choose a liquid base for your smoothie. I like to use coconut water, but all types of nut milks, rice milk and cow's milk work fantastically well also. I use about 500 ml (17 fl oz/2 cups), but you can add a little more or less depending on the thickness desired.

◆ Next, I like to add something a little creamy, and also a good dose of healthy fats. I usually add an avocado, or 125 ml (4 fl oz/½ cup) coconut cream; some nut butter, or a handful of nuts that have been soaked overnight (to make them easier to digest) add a terrific dimension also.

◆ Time to choose a few handfuls of fruit! I usually opt for 2 frozen bananas, as I always have an abundance in the freezer. Frozen grapes, apples, figs and berries are also a perfectly sweet addition, and if I'm wanting something tropical I'll add some mango or pineapple. Feijoas, also pictured, make a lovely addition when in season.

◆ Last but not least, add a large handful or portion of greens. Some great options are spinach, kale, cos (romaine) lettuce, celery, broccoli, a bulb of fennel or ½ cucumber.

Once you have mastered the art of creating a delicious green smoothie combination, you can get a little fancy. Here are some ways to take your smoothie to the next flavour dimension.

◆ For a fresh 'zing', add the juice of ½ lemon or lime.

◆ Some herbs also make a nice addition, for example, a small handful of mint or parsley.

◆ Add some spices for extra health benefits — turmeric, ginger or a little pinch of cayenne pepper all work well.

◆ For a chilled and refreshing smoothie, I like to freeze my fruit or vegetables. If using your produce at room temperature, you can add a couple of ice cubes instead.

I hope you enjoy trying out some delicious flavour combinations!

a nourishing start to the day

a light & creamy
green smoothie

⟨◇◇◇◇◇◇◇◇⟩

recipe page 25

a lovely omelette with gruyère, red onion & fig jam

I love everything about this dish. This super-simple yet satisfying omelette is filled with oozy melted gruyère cheese, and topped with a dark and sticky red onion, balsamic and fig jam. It is wonderful served with a simple green herby salad for brunch.

SERVES 2 ◆ GF, VEG

For the red onion & fig jam
185 g (6½ oz/1 cup) dried figs
220 g (7¾ oz/1 cup) pitted prunes
4 red onions, cut into quarters
2 tablespoons extra virgin olive oil
2 tablespoons balsamic vinegar
2 tablespoons honey
1 teaspoon sea salt

For the omelette
4 free-range eggs
2 tablespoons ghee, butter
    or olive oil
50 g (1¾ oz) gruyère cheese,
    grated
chopped chives, to garnish
toasted seeds, for sprinkling
    (optional)

To make the jam, put the figs, prunes and onion in a food processor. Pulse for about 20 seconds, until well chopped.

Heat the olive oil in a large, heavy-based saucepan over medium–low heat. Add the chopped fig mixture and sauté for 2–3 minutes, or until soft.

Add the remaining jam ingredients and 750 ml (26 fl oz/3 cups) water. Bring to the boil, then reduce the heat to low and simmer for about 30 minutes, until the jam becomes thick and glossy.

Allow the jam to cool, then transfer to a sterilised 500 ml (17 fl oz/2 cup) jar; the jam will keep in the fridge for 2–3 weeks.

To prepare the omelette, crack the eggs into a mixing bowl, add a good pinch of sea salt and freshly ground black pepper and mix well.

Heat the ghee in a large frying pan over medium heat. Add the eggs, swirling the pan around to spread the egg mixture evenly. After about 3 minutes, when the omelette begins to cook and firm up, but still has a little raw egg on top, sprinkle the grated cheese over.

Using a spatula, carefully lift up the edges of the omelette and fold it over in half. Cook for a further minute or two, then when the bottom starts to turn slightly golden, carefully slide the omelette onto a plate.

Sprinkle with chives, and toasted seeds if desired. Slice in half and share between two, with a good dollop of your lovely jam.

a nourishing start to the day

buttermilk breakfast bread with honey

*There is something so beautiful and comforting about using your own hands to create
a wholesome loaf of warm, sweet deliciousness. The dough can be prepared the night before
and then baked in the morning, filling the house with the loveliest aromas. The buttermilk
in this recipe adds a buttery richness and slight tang, similar to yoghurt. We like to enjoy
the bread fresh from the oven, although it also makes a wonderful sandwich bread,
and can even be made into small rolls.*

MAKES 1 LOAF, OR 8–10 ROLLS ◆ GF (using buckwheat flour), VEG

60 ml (2 fl oz/¼ cup) warm water
(the temperature of a bath)
1 teaspoon honey
2 teaspoons active dried yeast
375 ml (13 fl oz/1½ cups)
warm buttermilk, or 250 g
(9 oz/1 cup) plain yoghurt and
125 ml (4 fl oz/½ cup) water
115 g (4 oz/⅓ cup) honey
1 teaspoon sea salt
400 g (14 oz/4 cups) spelt flour,
or 520 g (1 lb 2½ oz/4 cups)
buckwheat flour,
plus extra for kneading
1 egg, lightly beaten, or
2 tablespoons milk, for brushing

Combine the water, honey and yeast in a small bowl and stir together
lightly. Leave to sit for about 10 minutes, or until foamy.

Put the remaining ingredients, except the beaten egg, in a large bowl.
Add the yeast mixture and, using a fork, mix until the dough starts to
come together.

Turn out onto a floured surface and knead softly for a few minutes until
smooth — the dough should be firm, but still slightly sticky. You can shape
it into a ball if you like. Place in an oiled bowl, then cover with a damp
tea towel (dish towel). Leave to rise in a warm place for at least 2 hours,
or overnight.

Punch the dough down to remove the excess air, then place in a greased
loaf (bar) tin that is about 12 cm (4½ inches) wide, 23 cm (9 inches) long,
and 7 cm (2¾ inches) deep. Using a sharp knife, score the dough two or
three times. Brush the top of the loaf with the egg, then leave the bread
to rise again for at least another 30–40 minutes.

Meanwhile, preheat the oven to 190°C (375°F).

Transfer the bread to the oven and bake for 45 minutes, or until it is
slightly browned and sounds hollow when tapped on the bottom. Remove
from the oven and turn out onto a wire rack. Leave to cool for 15 minutes
before slicing.

The bread will keep for 2–3 days in an airtight container, and can be frozen
for up to 2 months.

ricotta scrambled eggs
with spring onion

*Ricotta cheese adds a beautiful light creaminess to this slightly fancier version
of scrambled eggs. A lovely breakfast dish, it also works wonderfully as a simple
summer dinner, served with a leafy green salad and a few slices of ripe avocado,
or some cherry tomatoes tossed with chopped fresh basil and a good drizzle
of extra virgin olive oil.*

SERVES 4 ◆ GF, VEG

3 tablespoons ghee, butter or
   olive oil
8 free-range eggs, lightly whisked
250 g (9 oz/1 cup) ricotta cheese
4 spring onions (scallions),
   finely chopped

Heat the ghee in a large frying pan over medium heat. Add the eggs,
then leave for a minute or two, stirring once or twice, until almost cooked.

Remove from the heat, season with sea salt and freshly ground black
pepper, then gently stir in the ricotta and spring onion. The eggs will
continue to cook from the heat of the pan.

Serve immediately.

lovingly made
milk pudding with figs

*This simple hot breakfast has a base of brown rice flakes, giving it an
extraordinarily light and creamy finish. I like to make it with whole organic milk,
although coconut milk or nut milk would also work well if you are dairy free.*

SERVES 4 ◆ GF, DF (using nut or coconut milk), VEG, V (if no dairy milk or honey used)

500 ml (17 fl oz/2 cups) full-cream
   (whole) organic milk, or
   dairy-free milk of your choice
2 teaspoons vanilla bean paste
   or pure vanilla extract
200 g (7 oz/2 cups) brown
   rice flakes
sliced dried figs, to serve
honey or maple syrup, for drizzling

Add the milk, vanilla and rice flakes to a saucepan. Stir gently over
medium heat for 1–2 minutes, or until the mixture comes to a light simmer.

Remove from the heat, then allow the pudding to sit for 1–2 minutes, or
until the rice flakes have softened.

Divide among four bowls. Top with a few dried fig slices, drizzle with
honey and serve.

hot chocolate for a cold morning

In winter, home-made hot chocolate is quite often requested by the little ones. After heating the milk on the stovetop, I give it a quick blitzing in a blender, along with a little honey and good-quality cocoa powder, for a thick, creamy finish. Once you try this recipe, I promise the café-bought variety will pale in comparison.

SERVES 4 ◆ GF, DF (using nut or coconut milk), VEG, V (if no dairy milk or honey used)

1 litre (35 fl oz/4 cups) full-cream (whole) organic milk, or dairy-free milk of your choice
2 heaped tablespoons good-quality unsweetened cocoa powder, plus extra for sprinkling
2 tablespoons honey, or maple or brown rice syrup
2 teaspoons pure vanilla extract

Pour the milk into a small saucepan and warm over medium heat until steaming.

Carefully pour the milk into a blender. Add the remaining ingredients and blend for 20–30 seconds, until slightly frothy and creamy.

Pour into warm mugs, sprinkle with extra cocoa and enjoy!

cinnamon oatmeal
cooked in pure apple juice

*The oats in this comforting hot porridge are cooked in pure apple juice and
delicately spiced with a little cinnamon. Each mouthful is something quite
magical, the flavours melting together and working in perfect harmony.
For pure indulgence on a cold winter's morning, I serve ours with a
splash of thin (pouring/whipping) cream.*

SERVES 4 ◆ GF (using GF oats), DF (using nut or coconut milk), VEG,
V (using nut or coconut milk)

200 g (7 oz/2 cups) organic rolled
(porridge) oats
1 litre (35 fl oz/4 cups)
unsweetened apple juice; you
can use half water, half apple
juice if you prefer it less sweet
a pinch of sea salt
cream or dairy-free milk of your
choice, for drizzling
ground cinnamon, for sprinkling

Add the oats, apple juice and sea salt to a saucepan. Bring to a soft
boil over medium heat, then leave to simmer for a minute or so, stirring
until the desired consistency is reached.

Remove from the heat and leave to sit for 1–2 minutes.

Divide among bowls, then drizzle with your choice of milk or cream.
Sprinkle with cinnamon and serve.

coconut & dried plum breakfast bars

*Gloriously fudgy, these little bars are great for a quick breakfast on the run.
In this version I have used dried plums, which I picked up from my local
organic store, although figs, dates or apricots also work superbly.*

MAKES ABOUT 12 ◆ GF (using GF oats), DF, VEG, V

185 g (6½ oz/1 cup) dried plums,
  or dried fruit of your choice
200 g (7 oz/2 cups) organic
  rolled (porridge) oats; rice or
  quinoa flakes also work well
  for a gluten-free option
185 ml (6 fl oz/¾ cup) coconut
  cream
125 ml (4 fl oz/½ cup) melted
  coconut oil
35 g (1¼ oz/¼ cup) coconut or
  muscovado sugar
zest of 1 lemon
1 teaspoon pure vanilla extract
60 g (2¼ oz/1 cup) shredded
  coconut, plus a little extra
  for topping

Add the dried fruit to a food processor and pulse until roughly chopped.
Add the remaining ingredients and blend until combined.

Find a slab tin measuring about 24 x 20 cm (9½ x 8 inches) and line it
with baking paper. Press the mixture evenly into the tin, then top with
a little extra shredded coconut. Press down slightly.

Leave to set in the freezer for at least 1 hour, before slicing into bars.

The bars will keep in an airtight container for up to 1 week and are best
kept in the fridge.

a nourishing start to the day

yoghurt bowls with almond pangrattato & berry jam

These pretty little yoghurt bowls are a perfectly light breakfast, morning tea or even afternoon tea in the summer time. The creamy yoghurt is perfectly balanced with crunchy home-made almond crumbs and naturally sweetened berry jam. The recipe makes a small jar full of pangrattato, which can be enjoyed for a couple of weeks. You could use coconut yoghurt instead of plain yoghurt if you are dairy-free.

SERVES 4 ◆ GF, DF (using coconut yoghurt), VEG, V (if no dairy yoghurt or honey used)

For the berry jam
70 g (2½ oz/½ cup) fresh or frozen
    berries of your choice
90 g (3¼ oz/¼ cup) honey, or
    60 ml (2 fl oz/¼ cup) maple
    syrup or brown rice syrup
juice of ½ lemon

For the almond pangrattato
235 g (8½ oz/1½ cups) almonds,
    toasted
110 g (3¾ oz/¾ cup) coconut sugar

To serve
250 g (9 oz/1 cup) plain yoghurt
    or coconut yoghurt
fresh fruit, thinly sliced

To make the jam, add the berries, honey and 60 ml (2 fl oz/¼ cup) water to a small saucepan. Bring to a soft boil over medium heat, then leave to simmer for 15–20 minutes, or until the berries are soft and pulpy. Stir in the lemon juice, then leave to cool completely.

To make the pangrattato, add the toasted almonds and coconut sugar to a food processor. Blend until a rough breadcrumb consistency is achieved. Transfer to an airtight container or sterilised jar until required; the pangrattato will keep for up to 1 month.

To serve, divide the yoghurt and fresh fruit among four bowls. Add a dollop of the berry jam and a generous sprinkle of the pangrattato and serve.

roasted hazelnut & chocolate spread with sea salt

This perfectly rustic and chunky sweet delight is delicious smeared generously over a piece of sourdough toast, eaten as a dip with fresh apple or pear slices, or simply enjoyed straight from the spoon! The recipe accommodates all sorts of variations. I have made it using almonds, pecans and cashew nuts, and all taste divine; you could also add some spices to fancy it up.

MAKES ABOUT ONE 500 ML (17 FL OZ/2 CUP) JAR ◆ GF, DF, VEG, V (if no honey used)

280 g (10 oz/2 cups) raw hazelnuts
sea salt, for sprinkling
60 g (2¼ oz/½ cup) good-quality
 unsweetened cocoa powder
115 g (4 oz/⅓ cup) honey, or 80 ml
 (2½ fl oz/⅓ cup) maple syrup
 or brown rice syrup
90 g (3¼ oz/⅓ cup) coconut oil
1 teaspoon pure vanilla extract

Preheat the oven to 180°C (350°F). Line a baking tray with baking paper.

Spread the hazelnuts in a single layer on the baking tray and sprinkle with sea salt. Roast for 10–12 minutes, checking once or twice and turning as needed. Once you start to smell a beautiful roasted nut fragrance, you can remove them from the oven. Leave to cool.

Transfer the hazelnuts to a food processor, along with the cocoa, honey, coconut oil and vanilla. Begin to process, slowly adding a scant 125 ml (4 fl oz/½ cup) water a little bit at a time, until the spread reaches your desired consistency.

Taste, and add a little more sweetener or sea salt as needed.

Transfer to a 500 ml (17 fl oz/2 cup) sterilised jar. The spread will keep in a cool, dark place for 3–4 weeks.

buckwheat drop scones with balsamic blackberry marbled yoghurt

These beautifully light little drop scones are best enjoyed straight from the pan.
The buckwheat flour gives a subtle earthy flavour — a perfect combination
with the tangy yoghurt.

MAKES 18–20 ◆ GF, VEG

For the marbled yoghurt
65 g (2¼ oz/½ cup) fresh
   or frozen blackberries
90 g (3¼ oz/¼ cup) honey, or
   60 ml (2 fl oz/¼ cup) maple
   syrup or brown rice syrup
juice of ½ lemon
250 g (9 oz/1 cup) plain yoghurt

For the scones
130 g (4½ oz/1 cup) buckwheat
   flour
80 g (2¾ oz/½ cup) rice flour
35 g (1¼ oz/¼ cup) coconut sugar
170 ml (5½ fl oz/⅔ cup) coconut
   milk or milk
2 free-range eggs
1 teaspoon bicarbonate of soda
   (baking soda)
½ teaspoon sea salt

To make the marbled yoghurt, add the blackberries, honey and 60 ml (2 fl oz/¼ cup) water to a small saucepan. Bring to a soft boil over medium heat, then leave to simmer for 15–20 minutes, or until the blackberries are soft and pulpy. Stir in the lemon juice, then leave to cool completely. Carefully marble the blackberry syrup through the yoghurt using a spoon.

Add all the scone ingredients to a food processor or blender, then whiz until smooth.

Lightly grease a large frying pan over medium-low heat. Now drop tablespoons of the batter into the pan, from the point of the spoon. As soon as little bubbles start to appear, turn the scones over, then continue to cook for a further minute or so on the other side, until golden.

Serve the scones warm, with a dollop of the marbled yoghurt.

a nourishing start to the day

sweet almond crepes with ricotta & honey grilled stone fruit

Perfect for a special occasion, these sweet breakfast crepes are filled with creamy ricotta cheese and sweet, juicy grilled stone fruit drizzled with honey and a little lemon juice. I like to make a double batch of crepes and have some spare in the fridge for quick and easy snacks. Just gorgeous.

MAKES 7–8 ◆ GF, VEG

For the filling
4 large nectarines or peaches,
    peeled and sliced into wedges
90 g (3¼ oz/¼ cup) honey
juice of ½ lemon
125 g (4½ oz/½ cup) ricotta cheese

For the crepes
5 free-range eggs
55 g (2 oz/½ cup) almond meal
2 tablespoons cornflour
    (cornstarch), or tapioca or
    potato starch
2 teaspoons honey
1 teaspoon pure vanilla extract
a pinch of sea salt

Preheat the oven to 180°C (350°F).

To make the filling, arrange the fruit in a baking dish, then drizzle with the honey and lemon juice. Bake for 20 minutes, or until the fruit has softened and is slightly caramelised. Remove from the oven and keep warm.

Meanwhile, add all the crepe ingredients to a food processor and blend until smooth.

Grease a large frying pan and place over high heat. Reduce the heat to low, then add 80 ml (2½ fl oz/⅓ cup) of the crepe batter to the pan, swirling the pan to coat the base. Cook the crepe for 1–2 minutes on each side, or until golden.

Repeat with the remaining batter, stacking the cooked crepes on top of each other and keeping them warm.

To serve, fill the crepes with the warm fruit and some ricotta. Enjoy warm.

moist banana &
nut-butter bread

*At our cafe in Auckland, called Mondays, this banana bread recipe is
requested often. Gorgeously moist, naturally sweet and insanely delicious,
it is perfection when toasted. It also keeps really well, and tastes even
better when it is a day or two old.*

MAKES 1 LOAF   ◆   GF (if no oat flour used), DF (if no butter used), VEG

3 ripe bananas, peeled
1 teaspoon pure vanilla extract
75 g (2½ oz/½ cup) rapadura,
   muscovado or coconut sugar
4 free-range eggs
1 teaspoon bicarbonate of soda
   (baking soda)
1 tablespoon apple cider vinegar
125 g (4½ oz/½ cup) nut butter
   (I like almond butter)
60 g (2¼ oz/¼ cup) coconut oil
   or butter
160 g (5½ oz/1 cup) rice flour,
   130 g (4½ oz/1 cup) buckwheat
   flour, or 90 g (3¼ oz/1 cup)
   oat flour

For the topping
2 bananas, sliced lengthways,
   for topping

Preheat the oven to 160°C (315°F). Find a loaf (bar) tin that is about
12 cm (4½ inches) wide, 23 cm (9 inches) long, and 7 cm (2¾ inches) deep.
Line it with baking paper.

Add all the ingredients, except the bananas for the topping, to a food
processor. Blend until smooth.

Pour the batter into the loaf tin, then top with the sliced bananas. Bake
for 45 minutes, or until a skewer inserted into the middle of the loaf
comes out clean.

Remove from the oven and turn out onto a wire rack. Leave to cool
completely, then cut into thick slices to serve.

The bread will keep for 4–5 days in an airtight container, and can be
frozen for up to 2 months.

a nourishing start to the day

vanilla & peanut butter granola

*My children, Bella and Obi, love this healthy granola. I like to whip up a big
batch on weekends, making a quick and nutritious breakfast option on school days,
served with fresh fruit and yoghurt or organic full-cream (whole) milk.*

MAKES 6–8 SERVES   ◆   GF (using GF oats), DF (using coconut oil), VEG, V (if no butter or honey used)

300 g (10½ oz/2 cups)
   wholegrain oats
125 g (4½ oz/½ cup) peanut butter
90 g (3¼ oz/¼ cup) honey, or
   60 ml (2 fl oz/¼ cup) maple
   syrup or brown rice syrup
60 g (2¼ oz/¼ cup) coconut oil
   or butter
3 teaspoons pure vanilla extract
a pinch of sea salt

Preheat the oven to 180°C (350°F). Line a baking tray with baking paper.

Add all the ingredients to a large mixing bowl and mix until well
combined. The mixture will be a little sticky!

Spread the granola out on the baking tray, in a single layer, about 1 cm
(½ inch) thick. Bake for 10–12 minutes, or until golden. Remove from the
oven and leave to cool.

The granola will keep in an airtight container for up to 1 month.

sweet coconut
& blackcurrant muffins

These marvellously moist muffins are naturally free of gluten, dairy and refined
sugar, and are sweetened with a touch of honey. The addition of coconut cream
gives a beautiful light and fluffy texture, although plain yoghurt works well too.
Lovely on a sunny Saturday morning with a big smear of organic butter.

MAKES 10 ◆ GF, DF (if no yoghurt used), VEG

185 ml (6 fl oz/¾ cup) coconut
   cream, or 200 g (7 oz/¾ cup)
   plain yoghurt
3 free-range eggs
125 g (4½ oz/½ cup) coconut oil
   or butter
90 g (3¼ oz/¼ cup) honey
160 g (5½ oz/1 cup) rice flour,
   or 130 g (4½ oz/1 cup)
   buckwheat flour
100 g (3½ oz/1 cup) almond meal
zest and juice of 1 lemon
1 teaspoon bicarbonate of soda
   (baking soda)
1 tablespoon apple cider vinegar
4 tablespoons frozen or fresh
   blackcurrants

Preheat the oven to 160°C (315°F). Grease 10 holes of a standard
muffin tin, or line with paper cases.

Add the coconut cream, eggs and coconut oil to a food processor.
Blend to a smooth batter.

Add the honey, flour, almond meal, lemon zest and lemon juice,
bicarbonate of soda and vinegar. Pulse again until well combined.

Gently fold the blackcurrants into the mixture, being careful not to
overmix. Divide the batter among the prepared muffin holes. Bake for
20–25 minutes, or until a skewer inserted into the centre of a muffin
comes out clean.

The muffins will keep for 2–3 days in an airtight container, and can
be frozen for up to 2 months.

chocolate rice puffs

This is most probably my kids' favourite recipe in this book! These chocolatey rice puffs are so delicious you won't believe they are good for you.

MAKES 8 SERVES ◆ GF, DF (if no butter used), VEG, V (if no butter used)

125 g (4½ oz/½ cup) coconut oil
    or butter
60 g (2¼ oz/½ cup) good-quality
    unsweetened cocoa powder
75 g (2½ oz/½ cup) rapadura,
    coconut or muscovado sugar
1 teaspoon pure vanilla extract
100 g (3½ oz/4 cups) unsweetened
    rice puffs

Preheat the oven to 150°C (300°F). Line two baking trays with baking paper.

Melt the coconut oil in a small saucepan over medium heat. Add the cocoa powder, sugar and vanilla, then whisk until dissolved. You will have a lovely thick, chocolatey sauce.

Put the rice puffs in a large mixing bowl. Pour the chocolate sauce over and mix until well coated.

Spread out the rice puffs on the baking trays, then pop into the oven. Turn off the heat completely, and leave them inside to crisp up slightly while the oven cools down.

The rice puffs will keep in an airtight container for 3–4 weeks.

gorgeous gingerbread
fudge smoothie

Fantastically wholesome, this smoothie has all the wonderful flavours of gingerbread, and is naturally sweetened with banana. Its star ingredient, ginger, is one I absolutely adore. Ginger is not only an amazing immune booster, but can also soothe an upset stomach and aid digestion. If your kids aren't so keen on the spice it brings, start off by adding half and, as they get used to it, you can add a little more.

SERVES 4 ◆ GF, DF (using almond milk), VEG, V (using almond milk and maple syrup)

3 bananas, frozen
750 ml (26 fl oz/3 cups) almond
　milk, or milk of your choice
90 g (3¼ oz/¼ cup) honey, or
　60 ml (2 fl oz/¼ cup) maple
　syrup
2 teaspoons apple cider vinegar
2 teaspoons pure vanilla extract
2 teaspoons ground ginger
1 teaspoon ground cinnamon
½ teaspoon ground nutmeg
8 ice cubes

Place all the ingredients in a blender and whiz together until smooth.

Pour into four glasses, then sprinkle with some extra spices if you like. Enjoy straight away.

incredible vegan
chocolate-chunk
cookies

◇◇◇◇◇◇◇◇◇

recipe page 84

ON
THE GO

Since having my children, I have learnt that it is necessary to always have plenty of wholesome and nutritious snacks on hand for school lunches, weekend picnics and hungry little tummies.

Whether it's little pots of yoghurt with a seasonal fruit compote, bite-sized free-range egg frittatas or brown butter cinnamon blondies for an indulgent treat, these home-made super snacks are bound to keep us all happy, fulfilled and full of energy.

simple savoury muffins

*Savoury muffins are a great opportunity to pack nutritious vegetables into
a tasty bake. Here is my favourite gluten-free base recipe — beautifully light,
fluffy and moist. I have added baby English spinach, basil and tomato,
although almost any grated vegetables would be equally delicious.*

MAKES 12 ◆ GF, DF, VEG

250 ml (9 fl oz/1 cup) coconut
   cream
125 ml (4½ fl oz/½ cup) olive oil
3 free-range eggs
1 teaspoon bicarbonate of soda
   (baking soda)
1 tablespoon apple cider vinegar
200 g (7 oz/2 cups) almond meal
160 g (5½ oz/1 cup) rice flour,
   or 150 g (5½ oz/1 cup)
   gluten-free flour
a handful of baby English spinach
   or shredded kale
a handful of basil leaves
2 tomatoes, sliced into 12 thin
   rounds

Preheat the oven to 160°C (315°F). Grease 12 holes of a standard
muffin tin, or line with paper cases.

Add all the ingredients, except the tomato, to a food processor or
blender. Season with sea salt and freshly ground black pepper, then
blend until smooth.

Pour the batter into the muffin holes, then top each with a tomato slice.
Bake for 20–25 minutes, or until a skewer inserted in the middle of a
muffin comes out clean.

The muffins will keep in an airtight container in a cool, dark place for
up to 2 days, and can be frozen for up to 1 month.

mini quiches with spinach & feta

A perfect savoury snack for kids' lunchboxes or when you're out and about, these gorgeous little bite-sized quiches are fantastically easy to prepare, and very adaptable. I sometimes add a little grated zucchini (courgette) or carrot for extra nourishment.

MAKES 8 ◆ GF, VEG

6 free-range eggs
a handful of baby English
   spinach leaves
1 onion, thinly sliced
75 g (2½ oz/½ cup) crumbled feta
   cheese, or 60 g (2¼ oz/½ cup)
   grated cheddar
a handful of pepitas (pumpkin
   seeds)

Preheat the oven to 180°C (350°F). Grease eight holes of a standard muffin tin, or line with paper cases.

In a large bowl, lightly beat the eggs. Add the spinach and onion and season with sea salt and freshly ground black pepper. Mix until combined.

Divide among the muffin holes and scatter the cheese and pepitas over the top. Bake for 20–25 minutes, or until a skewer inserted in the middle of a quiche comes out clean.

The quiches will keep in an airtight container in the fridge for up to 2 days, and can be frozen for up to 1 month.

potato & rosemary focaccias with roasted cherry tomatoes

Perfect as a picnic sandwich, this fragrant focaccia is made with mashed potato and spelt flour, although you could use buckwheat flour for a gluten-free alternative. With each mouthful, the baby tomatoes are little bursts of delight. I have also made this focaccia simply topped with rosemary and a little sea salt. Delicious!

MAKES ABOUT 12 SLICES ◆ GF (using buckwheat flour), VEG

1½ teaspoons dried yeast
230 g (8 oz/1 cup) cooked
    mashed potato
125 ml (4 fl oz/½ cup) olive oil
450 g (1 lb/4½ cups) spelt flour,
    or 585 g (1 lb 4½ oz/4½ cups)
    buckwheat flour, plus extra
    for kneading
1 teaspoon sea salt

For the topping
300 g (10½ oz/2 cups)
    cherry tomatoes
125 g (4½ oz) buffalo mozzarella,
    roughly chopped (grated
    mozzarella and most other
    cheeses also work well)
a large handful of fresh
    rosemary leaves

Pour 375 ml (13 fl oz/1½ cups) warm water into a large mixing bowl. Sprinkle the yeast over and leave for 5–10 minutes, or until frothy.

Mix in the mashed potato and olive oil. Stir in the flour and sea salt, and mix using your hands until the dough starts to come away from the side of the bowl. Turn the dough out onto a floured surface and knead for about 4–5 minutes.

Place the dough in a lightly oiled bowl, cover with plastic wrap and leave to rise for at least 3 hours, or overnight.

Preheat the oven to 200°C (400°F). Line two baking trays with baking paper.

Using oiled hands, separate the dough into two balls; the dough will be a little sticky. Using your hands, flatten the dough, then shape into a large rectangle measuring about 30 x 35 cm (12 x 14 inches), and about 1 cm (½ inch) thick. Repeat with the second ball of dough.

Top the bread bases with the whole cherry tomatoes and the cheese, then sprinkle with the rosemary and some sea salt and freshly ground black pepper.

Bake for 25 minutes, or until the tomatoes are well roasted, and the bread is nicely browned on the edges. Remove from the oven, and leave to cool before cutting into 12 pieces.

These focaccias are best enjoyed on the same day they are made.

crispy almond-coated chicken nuggets with home-made tomato sauce

Coated in a golden, crispy almond crumb, these chicken nuggets are wonderfully simple to prepare, and an absolute winner with the kids. I have also included my recipe for a super-speedy home-made tomato sauce, which is naturally sweetened with medjool dates. Totally delicious.

SERVES 2–3 ♦ GF, DF

2 free-range eggs
100 g (3½ oz/1 cup) almond meal
400 g (14 oz) skinless chicken
    breast fillets

For the home-made tomato sauce
400 g (14 oz) tin chopped
    tomatoes
4 tablespoons tomato paste
    (contentrated purée)
6 medjool dates, pitted
2 tablespoons honey

Add all the tomato sauce ingredients to a blender and whiz until smooth. Transfer to a small serving bowl, then season to taste with sea salt and freshly ground black pepper.

In a small bowl, lightly beat the eggs. Spread the almond meal on a plate. Cut the chicken into bite-sized pieces. Dip each piece into the egg, then coat in the almond meal.

Heat a chargrill pan to medium. Add the chicken and grill for 2–3 minutes on each side, or until the crumbs are lovely and golden and the chicken is cooked through.

Serve warm, with the tomato sauce for dipping into.

rainbow jars with
garlic-roasted hummus

*These vividly coloured picnic jars are an excellent way to get kids excited
about eating all the colours of the rainbow. The bottom of the jars are filled with
the most deliciously fragrant hummus, topped with seasonal vegetable sticks for
dipping into the hummus. When roasting the garlic, it's a great idea to roast some
other vegetables at the same time, to get the most benefit from your hot oven.*

MAKES ENOUGH FOR FOUR 300 ML (10½ FL OZ) JARS ◆ GF, DF, VEG, V

For the garlic-roasted hummus

2 whole garlic bulbs

80 ml (2½ fl oz/⅓ cup) extra virgin
  olive oil

a small handful of fresh thyme
  leaves

400 g (14 oz) tin chickpeas,
  rinsed and drained

juice of 1 lemon

2 tablespoons tahini (you can
  also use almond butter or
  peanut butter)

For the rainbow jars

a selection of seasonal vegetables,
  cut into thin sticks; carrot,
  capsicum (pepper), celery,
  cucumber and cherry tomatoes
  all work well

3 tablespoons toasted seeds;
  I use a mixture of pepitas
  (pumpkin seeds), sesame
  and sunflower seeds

Preheat the oven to 180°C (350°F).

To make the hummus, slice the tops off the garlic bulbs, so that the flesh
is exposed. Place in a small baking tray and drizzle with 2 tablespoons of
the olive oil. Sprinkle with a pinch of sea salt, then lay the thyme on top.

Bake for 45 minutes, or until the garlic cloves are soft and fragrant.
Remove from the oven and leave to cool.

Squeeze the garlic cloves out of their papery skins, into a food processor.
Add the remaining 2 tablespoons olive oil, the chickpeas, lemon juice,
tahini, and a pinch of sea salt and freshly ground black pepper. Process
until smooth. The hummus will keep in an airtight container in the fridge
for up to 1 week.

To assemble the rainbow jars, spoon 3–4 tablespoons of the hummus
into the bottom of four jars or pots. Arrange the vegetables on top, then
sprinkle with the toasted seeds.

If leaving at room temperature, serve within a few hours; the rainbow jars
can also be refrigerated for up to 1 day.

picnic frittata with cauliflower, cheddar & chives

Super-easy to make, this simple, rustic frittata is packed full of flavour, thanks to the addition of a few large handfuls of fresh herbs and a good hit of garlic. I make this frittata in a loaf tin, as it slices really easily, although you could also use a more traditional-style baking dish.

SERVES 4 ◆ GF, VEG

¼ head of cauliflower

8 free-range eggs

a large handful of English spinach, silverbeet (Swiss chard) or cavolo nero leaves, roughly chopped

2 large handfuls of fresh herbs; I use chives, thyme and flat-leaf (Italian) parsley

4 garlic cloves, roughly chopped

1 carrot, grated

a large handful of grated cheddar cheese

extra virgin olive oil, for drizzling

Preheat the oven to 180°C (350°F). Find a loaf (bar) tin that is about 12 cm (4½ inches) wide, 23 cm (9 inches) long, and 7 cm (2¾ inches) deep. Line it with baking paper.

Finely chop the cauliflower, or pulse it in a food processor.

In a large bowl, lightly beat the eggs. Add the cauliflower, spinach, herbs, garlic and carrot. Season with a good pinch of sea salt and freshly ground black pepper and mix until well combined.

Transfer the mixture to the loaf tin. Sprinkle with the grated cheese, then drizzle with olive oil.

Bake for 30–40 minutes, or until a skewer inserted in the middle of the frittata comes out clean. Remove from the oven and leave to cool before turning the frittata out of the tin. Cut into slices to serve.

The frittata will keep in an airtight container in the fridge for up to 2 days.

coconut cream & apricot bumper bars

These vegan bumper bars require no baking and only take a few minutes to prepare.
They have an awesome fudgy texture and make fantastic after-school snacks.

MAKES ABOUT 12 ◆ GF (using GF oats), DF, VEG, V

For the bars
180 g (6 oz/1 cup) dried apricots
200 g (7 oz/2 cups) rolled
    (porridge) oats (rice or quinoa
    flakes work well too)
60 g (2¼ oz/1 cup) shredded
    coconut
185 ml (6 fl oz/¾ cup) coconut
    cream
125 ml (4 fl oz/½ cup) melted
    coconut oil
35 g (1¼ oz/¼ cup) rapadura,
    coconut or muscovado sugar
1 teaspoon ground cinnamon
1 teaspoon pure vanilla extract

For the topping
35 g (1¼ oz/¼ cup) cocoa nibs
15 g (½ oz/¼ cup) shredded
    coconut

Add the dried apricots to a food processor and pulse until roughly chopped. Add the remaining bar ingredients and blend until combined.

Press the mixture evenly into a slab tin lined with baking paper. Sprinkle with the cocoa nibs and shredded coconut.

Leave to set in the freezer for at least 1 hour before slicing into bars.

The bars will keep in an airtight container for 3–4 days and are best kept in the fridge.

fig shortbreads with olive oil & sea salt

These delicate little shortbreads are not too sweet and have a fantastic, slightly crumbly, texture. They are magical dipped into a mug of tea or warm milk, melting into deliciousness as they disappear.

MAKES ABOUT 12 ◆ GF, DF, VEG, V

100 g (3½ oz/1 cup) almond meal
125 g (4½ oz/½ cup) peanut, almond or cashew butter
80 g (2¾ oz/½ cup) pitted medjool dates
80 g (2¾ oz/½ cup) dried figs
60 ml (2 fl oz/¼ cup) olive oil
1½ teaspoons pure vanilla extract
½ teaspoon bicarbonate of soda (baking soda)
sea salt, for sprinkling

Preheat the oven to 160°C (315°F). Line two baking trays with baking paper.

Put all the ingredients, except the sea salt, in a food processor. Pulse until a dough-like texture is achieved — this usually takes a couple of minutes, and you may need to scrape down the side of the processor now and then.

Shape the dough into a ball, wrap in plastic wrap and leave to rest in the fridge for 15 minutes.

Place the dough on a large piece of baking paper on a work surface. Using a rolling pin, roll out the dough to about 1 cm (½ inch) thick. Using the rim of a small glass or cookie cutter, cut out small rounds and place carefully on the baking trays. You may need to roll out the dough two or three times to use it all.

Sprinkle the shortbreads liberally with sea salt, then transfer to the oven and bake for 12–15 minutes, or until nice and golden on the outside. Remove from the oven and leave to cool on the baking tray.

The shortbreads will keep in an airtight container in a cool, dark place for 3–4 days.

little pots of yoghurt with plum & orange juice compote

My children, Bella and Obi, love plain yoghurt, and enjoy a little bowl full each day. I jazz it up by making seasonal fruit compotes that I can dollop on top. This plum version is cooked in pure orange juice and has a hint of spice. It is bright, zesty and delicious, and the kids can't get enough of it.

SERVES 4 ◆ GF, DF (using coconut yoghurt), VEG, V (if no honey or dairy yoghurt used)

1 kg (2 lb 4 oz) red plums, halved
    and pitted
175 g (6 oz/½ cup) honey, or
    125 ml (4 fl oz/½ cup) maple
    syrup or brown rice syrup
750 ml (26 fl oz/3 cups) freshly
    squeezed orange juice
½ teaspoon ground allspice
½ teaspoon ground cinnamon
500 g (1 lb 2 oz/2 cups) plain
    yoghurt, or coconut yoghurt

In a large saucepan, combine the plums, honey, orange juice, allspice and cinnamon. Bring to a soft boil over medium heat, then simmer on low for 25–30 minutes, or until almost all the liquid has cooked off and the plums are thick and jammy. Set aside to cool completely.

To serve, divide the yoghurt among serving jars or bowls, then dollop with the compote. Swirl to marble the compote through the yoghurt.

brown butter cinnamon blondies

I love seeing the pure delight on my little ones' faces as they bite into these delicious brown butter blondies. A blondie is basically a caramel version of a brownie, with the same incredible fudge texture.

MAKES 12 ◆ GF (if no spelt flour used), DF (using cocoa butter), VEG

For the blondies

170 g (6 oz/⅔ cup) unsalted butter or cocoa butter

150 g (5½ oz/1½ cups) spelt flour, 195 g (6¾ oz/1½ cups) buckwheat flour, 240 g (8½ oz/1½ cups) brown rice flour, or 180 g (6 oz/1½ cups) quinoa flour

150 g (5½ oz/1 cup) rapadura, coconut or muscovado sugar

2 free-range eggs

2 teaspoons pure vanilla extract

1 teaspoon bicarbonate of soda (baking soda)

a pinch of sea salt

For dusting

1 teaspoon ground cinnamon

35 g (1¼ oz/¼ cup) rapadura, coconut or muscovado sugar

Preheat the oven to 160°C (315°F). Find a baking dish measuring about 24 x 20 cm (9½ x 8 inches) and line it with baking paper.

If using butter, brown the butter by melting it in a frying pan over low heat and cooking until it is golden and smells deliciously nutty, then set aside to cool. If using cocoa butter, skip this process.

Add the remaining blondie ingredients to a food processor, then blend until smooth. Add the melted butter or cocoa butter and blend until just combined, then pour the batter into the baking dish.

In a small bowl, mix the cinnamon and sugar together, then sprinkle evenly over the blondie mixture.

Transfer to the oven and bake for 30–40 minutes, or until a skewer inserted in the middle comes out clean. Remove from the oven and leave to cool, then slice into bars.

The blondies will keep in an airtight container in a cool, dark place for 3–4 days.

incredible vegan chocolate-chunk cookies

*Who doesn't love a fabulous chocolate-chunk cookie? These wholesome cookies are made with
oat flour, although you could also use buckwheat, amaranth or quinoa flour if you prefer.
This is my go-to recipe for when we have young guests coming over.*

MAKES 12 LARGE COOKIES ◆ GF, DF (if no butter used), VEG, V (if no butter or egg used)

250 g (9 oz/2½ cups) gluten-free
    rolled (porridge) oats
1 teaspoon bicarbonate of soda
    (baking soda)
a pinch of sea salt
110 g (3¾ oz/¾ cup) rapadura,
    muscovado or coconut sugar
125 ml (4 fl oz/½ cup) melted
    coconut oil or butter
1 linseed egg (see note), or
    1 free-range egg
1 teaspoon pure vanilla extract
150 g (5½ oz/1 cup) roughly
    chopped good-quality
    dark chocolate

Preheat the oven to 160°C (315°F). Line two baking trays with
baking paper.

Place the oats in a food processor and chop until they have a super-fine
consistency, similar to flour. You may need to scrape down the side of
the processor with a spatula every now and then. Add the remaining
ingredients, then blend until the mixture comes together like a dough.

Using your hands, roll large handfuls of the dough into balls and place
them 3–4 cm (1¼–1¾ inches) apart on the baking trays. Press each ball
in half to flatten them into cookies.

Bake for 10–12 minutes, or until the cookies are slightly golden brown
on the edges. Remove from the oven and leave to cool on the trays.

The cookies will keep in an airtight container in a cool, dark place
for 3–4 days.

note

To make a linseed egg, mix 1 tablespoon ground linseed (flaxseed)
with 60 ml (2 fl oz/¼ cup) water in a small bowl. The mixture will start
to get thick and gluggy, with an egg-like consistency.

Recipe photograph on page 60

apricot, coconut & lemon snack bars

These apricot snack bars are amazingly simple and fast to prepare, and require no cooking.
They are naturally sweetened, making them great for sustained energy throughout the day.
This recipe uses almond meal, but ground seeds would also work well. You could also roll
the mixture into bite-sized balls, making them a little more enjoyable for the kids.

MAKES ABOUT 9 ✦ GF, DF, VEG, V

150 g (5½ oz/1½ cups) almond meal
180 g (6 oz/1 cup) dried apricots
60 g (2¼ oz/1 cup) shredded
    coconut
juice of 1 lemon

Simply place all the ingredients in a food processor and whiz until
the mixture starts to come together.

Line a small tray with baking paper, and press the mixture in evenly.
Place in the fridge to set for a couple of hours, then slice into bars.

These bars are best kept in the fridge. They will keep in an airtight
container for up to 1 week.

Recipe photograph on page 86

apricot, coconut
& lemon snack bars

◇◇◇◇◇◇◇◇◇

recipe page 85

pumpkin, hazelnut & date cookies with chocolate drizzle

Subtly spiced with cinnamon, and drizzled with a home-made dark chocolate sauce, these cookies are enticingly soft and chewy. You could also make them using banana instead of pumpkin, if you prefer, and replace the hazelnut with other nuts, such as almonds.

MAKES ABOUT 15 ◆ GF, DF, VEG

220 g (7¾ oz/2 cups) ground hazelnuts, or other ground nuts of your choice
1 teaspoon ground cinnamon
160 g (5½ oz/1 cup) pitted medjool dates
125 g (4½ oz/½ cup) cooked pumpkin (squash) purée
½ teaspoon bicarbonate of soda (baking soda)
1 tablespoon apple cider vinegar

For the chocolate drizzle
60 g (2½ oz/¼ cup) coconut oil
2 tablespoons honey
2 tablespoons good-quality unsweetened cocoa powder
1 teaspoon pure vanilla extract

Preheat the oven to 160°C (315°F). Line a baking tray with baking paper.

Add the hazelnut meal, cinnamon, dates, pumpkin purée, bicarbonate of soda and vinegar to a food processor. Blend until the mixture begins to come together like a dough.

Using your hands, roll the mixture into small balls and place them on the baking tray. Press on each ball lightly, to form a flat cookie shape.

Bake for 12 minutes, or until lightly golden, keeping an eye on them towards the end of cooking, as they can burn easily on the bottom.

Remove from the oven and turn out onto a wire rack to cool, so they don't keep cooking underneath.

To make the chocolate drizzle, put the coconut oil and honey in a saucepan and melt together over very low heat. Add the cocoa powder and vanilla and whisk until smooth. Remove from the heat and leave to cool slightly; the sauce will thicken a little.

Using a spoon, drip the chocolate drizzle over the cookies. Place the cookies in the fridge to set for 10–20 minutes before eating.

The cookies will keep for 2–3 days in an airtight container in the fridge.

ginger cookie dough truffles

I really love whipping up these incredible truffles. They take all of five minutes to make, and have the most brilliant cookie-dough texture. The trick is to use medjool dates instead of regular dried dates, as they have the most decadent and sweet caramel texture.

MAKES ABOUT 20 ◆ GF, DF, VEG, V

160 g (5½ oz/1 cup) pitted
    medjool dates
100 g (3½ oz/1 cup) almond meal
2 teaspoons ground ginger
80 g (2¾ oz/⅓ cup) nut butter
    (I like almond, but peanut is
    also lovely!)
2 tablespoons coconut oil

Add all the ingredients to a food processor, then blend for a minute or so, until the mixture starts to come together like a dough.

Using your hands, roll into small balls.

The truffles will keep in an airtight container in a cool, dark place for 3–4 days.

divine lemony almond cakes

These lovely little almond cakes have a fantastic citrus zing, and a nice, moist texture from the ground nuts. If I am feeling a little fancy, I like to ice them with whipped coconut cream or pure mascarpone cheese — but they are also quite wonderful just as they are.

MAKES 8 ◆ GF, DF (if using coconut oil), VEG

3 free-range eggs
90 g (3¼ oz/¼ cup) honey, or
   60 ml (2 fl oz/¼ cup) maple
   syrup or agave syrup
80 ml (2½ fl oz/⅓ cup) melted
   coconut oil or butter
grated zest of 2 lemons
1 teaspoon bicarbonate of soda
   (baking soda)
1 teaspoon apple cider vinegar
200 g (7 oz/2 cups) almond meal

Preheat the oven to 160°C (315°F). Grease eight holes of a standard muffin tin, or line with paper cases.

Add the eggs, honey, coconut oil, lemon zest, bicarbonate of soda and vinegar to a food processor or blender. Process for a minute or so, until your have a smooth, creamy batter.

Place the almond meal in a large mixing bowl. Pour in the batter and fold it through until well combined.

Spoon the batter into the muffin holes and bake for 25 minutes, or until a skewer inserted into the middle of a cake comes out clean.

These cakes will keep for 2–3 days in an airtight container, or can be frozen for up to 2 months.

oat slice sweetened with jam

*Naturally sweetened with berry jam, this delicious slice contains
just a handful of simple ingredients. Feel free to add your favourite
dried fruits, nuts or seeds. My daughter likes to place the slice in
the freezer for a fudgy frozen treat.*

MAKES ABOUT 9 SLICES ◆ GF (using GF oats), DF (using coconut oil), VEG

185 g (6½ oz/¾ cup) nut butter
(I often use cashew)
160 g (5½ oz/½ cup) naturally
sweetened jam (see note)
60 g (2¼ oz/¼ cup) coconut oil
or butter
60 g (2¼ oz/1 cup) shredded
or desiccated coconut
150 g (5½ oz/1½ cups) rolled
(porridge) oats, or you can
use millet, rice or quinoa flakes
if you prefer
2 free-range eggs

Preheat the oven to 170°C (325°F). Find a slab tin measuring about
24 x 20 cm (9½ x 8 inches) and line it with baking paper.

Place all the ingredients in a large mixing bowl. Using your hands,
mix until well combined. Press the mixture into the tin.

Bake for 20 minutes, or until golden on top. Remove from the oven
and leave to cool completely in the tin before slicing.

The slice will keep in an airtight container in the fridge for 2–3 days.

note

I use home-made jam, made with organic berries, a little water, honey,
chia seeds and a dash of lemon. You can usually find naturally sweetened
brands at the supermarket also.

coconut flour bars with dark chocolate chunks

It's great being able to make simple but healthy baked goods for children's lunchboxes, as you can be sure they will be nourishing and full of natural ingredients. I've added a little good-quality dark chocolate to these wholesome bars. My daughter absolutely loves them.

MAKES 12 ◆ GF, DF, VEG

125 ml (4 fl oz/½ cup) melted coconut oil

150 g (5½ oz/1 cup) rapadura, muscovado or coconut sugar

2 teaspoons pure vanilla extract

4 free-range eggs

170 ml (5½ fl oz/⅔ cup) coconut cream

120 g (4¼ oz/1 cup) coconut flour, plus extra for dusting

1 teaspoon bicarbonate of soda (baking soda)

a pinch of sea salt

100 g (3½ oz) good-quality dark chocolate, roughly chopped

Preheat the oven to 160°C (315°F). Find a baking dish measuring about 24 x 20 cm (9½ x 8 inches) and line it with baking paper.

In a large bowl, combine all the ingredients, except the chocolate. Mix until well combined, then fold in the chocolate pieces.

Spoon the mixture into the baking dish, smoothing it out evenly. Bake for 30–35 minutes, or until the outer edges are crispy and the inner portion is slightly firm, but still soft to touch. The mixture may seem a little undercooked, but will continue to cook as it cools down.

Leave to cool in the baking dish for at least 15–20 minutes. Dust with a light coating of extra coconut flour. Slice, then enjoy!

The bars will keep in an airtight container in a cool, dark place for 2 days.

brown butter apple cakes

The beautiful sweet fragrance that wafts through the kitchen as these cakes are baking is absolutely out of this world. Browning the butter before folding it into the cake batter gives the most incredible nutty aroma! Naturally gluten-free, these cakes have a moist, rich texture and are lightly sweetened with honey. I like to eat them warm, with a little dollop of whipped cream.

MAKES 8 ◆ GF, DF (using coconut oil and non-dairy milk), VEG

100 g (3½ oz) unsalted butter
  or coconut oil
100 g (3½ oz/1 cup) almond meal
80 g (2¾ oz/½ cup) brown rice
  flour (see note)
1 teaspoon bicarbonate of soda
  (baking soda)
1 teaspoon ground nutmeg
1 tablespoon apple cider vinegar
2 free-range eggs
90 g (3¼ oz/¼ cup) honey, or
  60 ml (2 fl oz/¼ cup) maple
  syrup or brown rice syrup
60 ml (2 fl oz/¼ cup) milk of
  your choice
1 apple, thinly sliced into wedges

Preheat the oven to 180°C (350°F). Grease eight holes of a standard muffin tin, or line with paper cases.

Melt the butter in a small saucepan over medium heat, then let it simmer until it has browned and has a beautiful nutty fragrance. (If you're using coconut oil, just gently melt it in the pan — there is no need to brown it.) Set aside to cool.

In a bowl, whisk together the almond meal, rice flour, bicarbonate of soda and nutmeg.

In a small bowl, whisk together the vinegar, eggs, honey and milk. Add the wet ingredients to the dry ingredients, then whisk to combine. Fold in the cooled browned butter.

Divide the batter among the muffin holes, filling them about three-quarters full, then top each with 2–3 apple wedges.

Bake for 15–20 minutes, or until golden brown on top. Remove from the oven and leave to cool on a wire rack.

The cakes will keep for 3–4 days in an airtight container, and can be frozen for up to 2 months.

note

Instead of rice flour you could use 65 g (2¼ oz/½ cup) buckwheat flour, 50 g (1¾ oz/½ cup) spelt flour (if not gluten-free), or an extra 50 g (1¾ oz/½ cup) almond meal if you prefer.

strawberry milk for the kids

*Fresh berries and a touch of honey naturally sweeten this delightful
flavoured milk. I use full-cream (whole) organic cow's milk, although
coconut or almond milk also work a dream. We like to fill up small
bottles to take with us to the park on a hot summer's day.*

SERVES 4 ◆ GF, DF (using coconut or almond milk), VEG

150 g (5½ oz/1 cup) fresh or
   frozen strawberries
90 g (3¼ oz/¼ cup) honey
1 litre (35 fl oz/4 cups) milk
   of your choice

Add all the ingredients to a blender and whiz until smooth.

Strain through a fine-meshed sieve. Serve chilled.

chickpea
flour pizzas

◇◇◇◇◇◇◇◇◇

recipe page 111

FOR
SHARING

The recipes in this chapter are designed for almost any type of gathering or occasion.

A few of my favourites worth mentioning are the fantastically crispy chickpea flour pizzas, which are perfect for a delicious weekend lunch; a vibrant, exciting tasting platter just perfect for eating outside in summer; and a gorgeous zesty pineapple hummingbird cake, which I love to make if I have friends coming over for afternoon tea.

I believe food is something that truly brings people together. I hope you enjoy sharing these recipes with those you love.

a spectacular platter

*One of my absolutely favourite ways to eat: a ridiculously large platter, scattered with
a spectacular array of colours and flavour combinations. It's all about variety here: crunchy
from the raw vegetables, crisp and salty roasted kale, warm roasted hazelnut vegetables,
a zingy lemon dipping oil and a beautifully creamy anchovy aïoli.*

SERVES 6–8 AS A TASTING PLATTER, OR 4 AS A LIGHT MEAL ◆ GF, DF, VEG (if no anchovies used),
V (if no eggs or anchovies used)

8 baby carrots

8 baby beetroot (beets)

4 kale leaves, stems removed,
  leaves roughly chopped

extra virgin olive oil, for drizzling

4 free-range eggs, at room
  temperature

2 small radicchio or cos (romaine)
  lettuces, stem ends removed

1 red capsicum (pepper), cut into
  sticks about 1 cm (½ inch) thick

6 celery stalks, cut into small sticks

For the spice & seed mix

40 g (1½ oz/¼ cup) sesame seeds

30 g (1 oz/¼ cup) crushed
  hazelnuts

3 tablespoons fennel seeds

3 tablespoons cumin seeds

2 tablespoons poppy seeds

For the dipping oil

125 ml (4 fl oz/½ cup) extra virgin
  olive oil

juice of 3 lemons

1 tablespoon dijon mustard

For the creamy cashew aïoli

235 g (8½ oz/1½ cups) cashew nuts

zest and juice of 1 lemon

60 ml (2 fl oz/¼ cup) olive oil

1 tablespoon apple cider vinegar

4 anchovies

Preheat the oven to 200°C (400°F).

Combine the spice and seed mix ingredients in a small bowl.

Arrange the carrots, beetroot and kale in a large roasting tin. Drizzle
generously with olive oil, then sprinkle with the seed mix. Bake for
25 minutes, or until the carrots and beetroot are cooked through and
the kale is crispy.

Meanwhile, bring a small saucepan of water to the boil, then carefully
add the eggs. Simmer for 7 minutes. Drain, then run under cold water
to cool. Carefully peel the eggs, then slice each egg in half.

Combine all the dipping oil ingredients in a small bowl. Season to taste
with sea salt and freshly ground black pepper.

Add all the aïoli ingredients to a blender, pour in a little less than 250 ml
(9 fl oz/1 cup) water and whiz until smooth; you may need to add a little
more water to achieve a lovely creamy consistency. Add a pinch of freshly
ground black pepper, then check the seasoning.

Arrange the roasted vegetables, raw vegetables and boiled eggs on
a large platter. Serve with the aïoli and dipping oil.

panzanella salad with lentils & sourdough

Panzanella is one of those fantastic stand-alone salads, with seriously robust flavours. It is best made towards the end of summer, when tomatoes are beautiful and ripe. I have added lentils to make the salad a little more substantial, and a small handful of roasted pepitas for a toasty crunch. One brilliant thing about this salad is that it becomes even more delicious when it has been made a few hours ahead. Something truly special happens to the flavours as they mingle and meld together.

SERVES 5–6 ◆ GF (using GF bread), DF, VEG (if no anchovies used), V (if no anchovies used)

400 g (14 oz) tin lentils, rinsed and drained (about 1½ cups cooked lentils)

½ loaf sourdough or gluten-free bread, cut into bite-sized cubes

500 g (1 lb 2 oz) tomatoes, roughly chopped

85 g (3 oz) jar of anchovies, drained and roughly chopped

a large handful of basil leaves

a large handful of oregano leaves

75 g (2½ oz/½ cup) sun-dried tomatoes, thinly sliced

125 ml (4 fl oz/½ cup) olive oil

60 ml (2 fl oz/¼ cup) balsamic vinegar

70 g (2½ oz/½ cup) pepitas (pumpkin seeds), lightly toasted (optional)

Add all the ingredients to a large bowl. Season with sea salt and freshly ground black pepper and toss until well combined.

If you have time, cover and set aside at room temperature for a few hours, for the flavours to merge.

chickpea flour pizzas

I'm not sure I know anyone who doesn't love pizza. It's the ultimate feel-good food, perfect for a casual lunch or dinner. These bases are so easy to make, and can be prepared faster than it would take to order in pizza. The chickpea flour gives the pizza a deeper, nuttier note and creates the most delicious golden crispy crust. I like to keep my toppings simple — home-made rich tomato sauce, fresh ricotta or mozzarella cheese, and a handful of earthy herbs. You can top yours with whatever takes your fancy.

MAKES 4 ◆ GF, DF (if no cheese used), VEG, V (if no cheese used)

For the pizza bases
120 g (4¼ oz/1 cup) chickpea flour, plus a little extra for kneading
130 g (4½ oz/1 cup) buckwheat flour
1 teaspoon bicarbonate of soda (baking soda)
1 teaspoon sea salt
60 ml (2 fl oz/¼ cup) melted coconut oil

For the topping
125 g (4½ oz/½ cup) Home-made tomato sauce (see page 70)
150 g (5½ oz) fresh ricotta cheese, or sliced mozzarella cheese
a handful of herbs, such as basil or thyme sprigs

Preheat the oven to 200°C (400°F). Line two large baking trays with baking paper.

To make the pizza bases, stir together the flours, bicarbonate of soda and sea salt in a mixing bowl. Add the coconut oil, and mix with a fork until well incorporated. Start adding about 185 ml (6 fl oz/¾ cup) warm water, a little at a time, until the mixture has a smooth consistency, being careful that the dough does not become too sticky.

Turn the dough out onto a floured surface and knead for 2 minutes. Cover with damp paper towel and leave to rest for 15 minutes.

Divide the dough into four balls, then roll each one out to about 5 mm (¼ inch) thick. Place two pizza bases on each baking tray. Spread each pizza base generously with the tomato sauce, then scatter with the cheese and sprinkle with herbs.

Bake for 8–10 minutes, or until the pizzas are nice and golden around the edges, and the toppings are well cooked. Serve hot.

creamy pesto butterbeans
with a simple salad

This is a big-flavoured dish with a loud and bright pesto dressing. We like
to eat this one outdoors on a summer's day, with a simple garden salad.

SERVES 4 AS A LIGHT LUNCH ◆ GF, DF (if no parmesan used), VEG, V (if no parmesan used)

2 x 400 g (14 oz) tins butterbeans,
   rinsed and drained

For the pesto
3 tablespoons nuts of your choice
a large handful of fresh basil or
   flat-leaf (Italian) parsley leaves
juice of 1 lemon
60 ml (2 fl oz/¼ cup) extra virgin
   olive oil
a small handful of grated
   parmesan cheese

For the salad
2–3 large handfuls of fresh
   salad leaves
extra virgin olive oil, for drizzling
juice of 1 lemon

To make the pesto, add the nuts, herbs, lemon juice, olive oil and parmesan to a food processor or blender. Blitz until a pesto-like consistency is achieved.

Put the pesto and butterbeans in a bowl and mix until nicely combined. Season to taste with sea salt and freshly ground black pepper.

Place the salad leaves in a bowl and drizzle with a little olive oil. Sprinkle with the lemon juice and a good pinch of salt and pepper. Toss lightly and serve with the butterbeans.

petite potato salad with cucumber & lemony crème fraiche

Potato salad is a family favourite, and this version is packed full of fragrant herbs, salty capers and an insanely delicious lemony crème fraîche dressing. This dish is an absolute crowd-pleaser.

SERVES 6–8 ● GF, VEG

1 kg (2 lb 4 oz) small new potatoes, scrubbed and sliced in half
1 telegraph (long) cucumber, sliced lengthways, then cut into thin slices
1 red onion, thinly sliced
a handful of capers, drained
2 large handfuls of mixed herbs; I use a mix of mint, oregano, chives and flat-leaf (Italian) parsley
250 g (9 oz/1 cup) crème fraîche (or sour cream if unavailable)
zest and juice of 2 lemons
extra virgin olive oil, for drizzling
30 g (1 oz/¼ cup) roughly ground hazelnuts

Place the potatoes in a large saucepan and cover with water. Add some salt and bring to the boil, then pop the lid on and turn off heat. Leave the potatoes to cook in the water until completely cooled.

Drain the potatoes well, then place in a large bowl (or two!), along with the cucumber, onion, capers and herbs.

In a small bowl, combine the crème fraîche, lemon zest and lemon juice. Stir in a good drizzle of olive oil and season with sea salt and freshly ground black pepper.

Drizzle the dressing over the potatoes and toss well to combine. Sprinkle the ground hazelnuts over the top.

Serve straight away, or cover and refrigerate for several hours and bring to room temperature for serving.

glorious pea, lemon & garlic guacamole packed with herbs

Here is a recipe for the most sensational guacamole. It contains plenty of lemon juice and zest for a citrus kick, a large handful of fresh herbs for extra vitality, a good drizzle of extra virgin olive oil, and some toasted seeds to give a fantastic rustic texture. A hint of chilli also wouldn't go amiss if that's your thing.

SERVES 4–6 ◆ GF, DF, VEG, V

6 tablespoons mixed pepitas (pumpkin seeds), sunflower seeds and sesame seeds

155 g (5½ oz/1 cup) fresh or frozen peas

2 perfectly ripe avocados

2 garlic cloves

a large handful of mixed herbs, such as mint, flat-leaf (Italian parsley) and oregano

zest and juice of 2 lemons

a good drizzle of extra virgin olive oil

Toast the seeds in a dry frying pan for a few minutes over medium heat, until fragrant. Set aside to cool slightly.

Steam or cook the peas for about 4 minutes, or until just tender, then drain and set aside to cool.

Put the seeds, peas and remaining ingredients in a food processor and blend for 30 seconds or so — I like my guacamole quite chunky, the more rustic the better.

Season to taste with sea salt and freshly ground black pepper. Serve straight away, or cover and refrigerate until serving time; the guacamole can be prepared several hours ahead.

barley, sweetcorn & avocado salad tossed with chilli lime dressing

This fantastically healthy salad is tossed with a punchy chilli lime dressing — a perfect summer dish, full of crunchy textures, vibrant colours and fresh bright flavours. I use barley in this salad as it has a pleasing chewy, slightly nutty texture, although quinoa, rice or most other grains would work well too; just adjust the cooking times accordingly.

SERVES 4 ◆ GF (using rice or quinoa), DF, VEG, V

220 g (7¾ oz/1 cup) barley;
   use rice or quinoa if you'd like
   the salad to be gluten-free)
4 cobs sweetcorn
1 red onion, diced
a large handful of fresh coriander
   (cilantro), roughly chopped
a large handful of flat-leaf (Italian)
   parsley, roughly chopped
1 teaspoon chilli powder, or
   chilli flakes
a good glug of extra virgin olive oil
juice of 2 limes
1–2 avocados, peeled and stoned,
   flesh chopped

Cook the barley or other grains according to the packet instructions. Drain and leave to cool.

Meanwhile, boil or steam the corn for about 10 minutes, or until just tender. Drain and leave to cool, then cut the kernels from the cobs using a sharp knife.

Place the cooled barley and corn in a bowl. Add the remaining ingredients and toss together, then season to taste with sea salt and freshly ground black pepper.

Serve straight away, or cover and refrigerate until serving time; the salad can be prepared several hours ahead.

figs & dates filled with salted almond butter

We often crave these sweet little treats in the afternoon — nutritious dried fruits filled with a rich, nutty almond butter. Use plump medjool dates here, for their deep caramel flavour. Dried figs are glorious too, with their unique sweet taste, soft chewy texture and deliciously crunchy edible seeds. My kids have decided they love these just as much as I do, which makes me very happy.

SERVES 4 AS A SNACK ◆ GF, DF, VEG, V

80 g (2¾ oz/½ cup) pitted
 medjool dates
95 g (3½ oz/½ cup) dried figs
60 g (2¼ oz/¼ cup) almond butter
flaky sea salt, to taste

Slice each date and fig open, and fill each with a teaspoon of almond butter. Sprinkle liberally with sea salt and serve.

glorious fruit kebabs

*I find as soon as I pop fruit or vegetables onto a wooden skewer and call it a
'kebab' the kids seem to go crazy for it! In this recipe, I have coated the fruit with
a lemon, maple and coconut oil syrup, which makes the fruit extra sweet and juicy
when grilled. This recipe is fantastic when you have a young crowd to please —
great for a kid's party or get together.*

MAKES 6–8   ◆   GF, DF, VEG, V

60 ml (2 fl oz/¼ cup) maple syrup
60 ml (2 fl oz/¼ cup) melted
   coconut oil
juice of 1 lemon
6 stone fruit of your choice —
   nectarines, peaches and apricots
   all work well

If using wooden skewers, soak them in water for at least 10 minutes, so they don't burn during grilling.

Combine the maple syrup, coconut oil and lemon juice in a bowl.

Slice each piece of fruit in half and remove the stones. Thread the fruit onto your skewers, alternating the different types for a colourful effect.

Heat a chargrill pan to medium–high heat. Using a pastry brush, paint the fruit with a light coating of the syrup mixture.

Cook the skewers for about 5 minutes, turning occasionally, until you have grill marks on all sides of the fruit. Serve warm.

iced rooibos tea with lemon,
honey & chia seeds

*When the sun is warm and bright, what could be more perfect to sip on than this
refreshing iced rooibos and honey tea, spiked with chia seeds and a hint of lemon.
Chia seeds are nature's superfood, packed full of calcium, omega-3 oils and antioxidants.
You might find the texture a little funny at first, but after a while you begin to love them.
Rooibos tea is my personal favourite, and it happens to be caffeine-free, so it's great for
kids — although green tea or black tea would also work well here. I often make up
a large pitcher filled with ice when we have guests over on weekends.*

SERVES 3–4 ◆ GF, DF, VEG

3–4 rooibos tea bags
2–3 tablespoons honey, or to taste
juice of ½ a lemon
3 tablespoons chia seeds
lemon slices, to serve (optional)

In a large glass pitcher or jar, place the tea bags, honey and lemon juice.
Top with 1–1.5 litres (35–52 fl oz/4–5 cups) boiling water and leave to
steep until warm.

Remove the tea bags, then stir in the chia seeds. Place in the fridge
for a few hours, until chilled.

Serve with a few slices of lemon if you desire.

rustic walnut & raisin tea bread

In colder weather, we tend to crave something warm, sweet and filling. Served fresh from the oven, this walnut fruit loaf hits the spot. Filled with soft, juicy raisins, this loaf is naturally sweetened with banana and a little honey. It slices beautifully, and has the most incredible texture. It also makes a great morning toast, simply smothered with butter, or topped with ricotta cheese and home-made jam. Feel free to add some spices, citrus zest or dried fruit of your choice.

MAKES 1 LOAF ◆ GF, DF (if no butter used), VEG

185 g (6½ oz/1½ cups) raisins; currants and sultanas (golden raisins) also work well

3 tea bags

230 g (8 oz/2 cups) ground walnuts (or other ground nuts of your choice)

5 free-range eggs

1 banana, roughly chopped

2 tablespoons honey

1 tablespoon coconut oil or butter

1 tablespoon apple cider vinegar

1 teaspoon bicarbonate of soda (baking soda)

a pinch of sea salt

Preheat the oven to 160°C (315°F). Find a loaf (bar) tin that is about 12 cm (4½ inches) wide, 23 cm (9 inches) long and 7 cm (2¾ inches) deep. Line it with baking paper.

Place the raisins and tea bags in a small saucepan and cover with water. Bring to a soft boil, then leave to simmer for 10–15 minutes, or until almost all the liquid has cooked off. Discard the tea bags and set aside.

Put the remaining ingredients in a food processor and blend until smooth.

Fold the raisins through the batter, then pour into the loaf tin, smoothing the surface evenly.

Bake for 30–45 minutes, or until a skewer inserted into the middle of the loaf comes out clean. Remove from the oven and leave to cool in the tin.

Slice into thick pieces, and enjoy with your favourite spread.

The loaf will keep for 3–4 days in an airtight container, and can be frozen for up to 2 months. For added convenience, slice the loaf before freezing.

spiced pumpkin scones

*Scones, wonderful scones. Perfectly buttery, crumbly, comforting and heavenly.
Pumpkin adds an incredible golden colour, with a delicious hum of warmth
from the spices. There is a magic hour after the scones have just come out
of the oven when they are so divine spread with a big smear of butter.
Perfect in the afternoon with a hot mug of tea.*

MAKES 16 ◆ GF (using GF flour), VEG

450 g (1 lb/4½ cups) spelt flour
    (see note)
75 g (2½ oz/½ cup) coconut or
    muscovado sugar
2 teaspoons bicarbonate of soda
    (baking soda)
½ teaspoon sea salt
1½ teaspoons ground cinnamon
1 teaspoon ground ginger
½ teaspoon ground nutmeg
250 g (9 oz) chilled unsalted
    butter, diced
2 free-range eggs
250 g (9 oz/1 cup) puréed cooked
    pumpkin (winter squash)
170 ml (5½ fl oz/⅔ cup) thin
    (pouring/whipping) cream or
    coconut cream, chilled

To finish
1 free-range egg, beaten
coconut or muscovado sugar,
    for sprinkling

Preheat the oven to 180°C (350°F). Line a baking tray with baking paper.

Add the flour, sugar, bicarbonate of soda, sea salt and spices to a food processor. Pulse to combine. Add the butter, then continue to pulse until the mixture resembles dense breadcrumbs.

In a bowl, lightly whisk the eggs. Stir in the pumpkin purée and cream. Add the mixture to the food processor and pulse until just combined. Small bits of butter should still be visible, but almost all the flour should be incorporated.

Turn the dough out onto a lightly floured surface. Working quickly, gently knead the dough, folding and pressing gently until fairly smooth.

Divide the dough into four portions, and flatten each piece into a round using your hands. Cut each round into four wedges and place on the baking tray. Brush each scone with the egg wash and sprinkle with coconut sugar.

Bake for about 15 minutes, or until the tops are lightly golden and the cut sides look flaky and dry. Be careful not to overcook them — you want them to be lovely and fluffy on the inside.

Remove from the oven and cool on a wire rack for at least 5 minutes. The scones are best served warm.

note ◇◇◇◇◇◇◇◇◇◇◇◇◇◇◇◇◇◇◇◇◇◇◇◇◇◇◇◇◇◇◇◇◇

You could use 4½ cups plain (all-purpose) gluten-free flour to make the recipe gluten-free. (We've simply given a cup measure here, as the gram or pound weight of the flour varies across different gluten-free brands.)

crepe birthday cake with lemon mascarpone & rosemary

I made this impressive crepe cake to celebrate my mum's birthday, and it was an absolute hit. Despite its striking appearance, it is surprisingly easy to pull together — although it does need a little patience and love to cook the mountain of crepes. Once you have completed the task, the assembly takes mere minutes and can be quite fun. A great one for getting the kids involved!

SERVES 10–12 ◆ GF, VEG

edible organic fresh flowers
  and herbs, to decorate

For the crepes
10 free-range eggs
320 g (11¼ oz/2 cups) rice flour
75 g (2½ oz/½ cup) coconut sugar
625 ml (21½ fl oz/2½ cups) almond
  milk, or milk of your choice
2 tablespoons finely chopped
  rosemary

For the mascarpone filling
660 g (1 lb 7 oz/3 cups)
  mascarpone cheese
zest and juice of 2 lemons
90 g (3¼ oz/¼ cup) honey, or
  60 ml (2 fl oz/¼ cup) maple
  syrup or brown rice syrup

Add all the crepe ingredients to a blender or food processor. Add a pinch of sea salt and blend until all the ingredients are well incorporated, and the batter is no longer lumpy. Transfer to a pitcher, to make pouring into the pan easier (my blender is a great pitcher already).

Combine the mascarpone filling ingredients in a bowl and mix well. Cover and set aside in the fridge.

To cook the crepes, place a greased frying pan over medium–low heat. With the batter in one hand and the hot pan in the other, slowly pour the batter into the pan, swirling the pan until there is enough batter to just coat the bottom of the pan. Cook for about 1 minute, or until the crepe is slightly browned at the edges, then flip with a spatula and brown on the other side. Flip onto a plate, then continue cooking the remaining batter in the same way.

To assemble the cake, place one crepe on the bottom of a serving plate. Spread a thin layer of the mascarpone filling over the crepe. Stack another crepe on top, then spread with more mascarpone filling. Continue the layers until you have nearly run out of the filling or crepes, whichever comes first!

Finish off the last crepe with a layer of the mascarpone mixture, and decorate with fresh flowers and herbs.

The crepe cake is best eaten the same day, but any leftovers will keep in an airtight container for up to 2 days. The crepes can also be cooked ahead and frozen, then thawed before the final filling and assembly.

the best banana cakes with mascarpone & roasted hazelnuts

When life calls for a delicious baked treat, these delightful little banana cakes
fit the bill. They have a delicate moist texture and a subtle hint of cinnamon.
I have only used ripe bananas and honey to naturally sweeten this recipe,
and topped them with mascarpone cheese for a simple creamy frosting.
This recipe can also be made as one large banana cake.

MAKES 12 ◆ GF (if no spelt used), VEG

For the cakes

4 ripe bananas

3 free-range eggs

170 ml (5½ fl oz/⅔ cup) melted
coconut oil or butter

200 g (7 oz/2 cups) almond meal

90 g (3¼ oz/⅔ cup) buckwheat
flour, 110 g (3¾ oz/⅔ cup)
rice flour, 80 g (2¾ oz/⅔ cup)
quinoa flour, or 65 g (2¼ oz/
⅔ cup) spelt flour

1½ teaspoons bicarbonate of soda
(baking soda)

1 tablespoon apple cider vinegar

1 teaspoon pure vanilla extract

175 g (6 oz/½ cup) honey

1 teaspoon ground cinnamon

For the topping

165 g (5¾ oz/¾ cup) mascarpone
cheese, approximately

35 g (1¼ oz/¼ cup) hazelnuts,
roasted (see note) and chopped

ground cinnamon, for sprinkling

edible organic fresh flowers

Preheat the oven to 160°C (315°F). Grease 12 holes of a standard muffin tin, or line with paper cases.

Add all the cake ingredients to a food processor and blend just until you have a smooth batter; take care not to overmix.

Divide the batter among the muffin holes and bake for 30–40 minutes, or until a skewer inserted in the middle of a cake comes out clean.

Remove from the oven and leave in the tin until completely cool, before carefully removing from the tin.

Top each cake with about a tablespoon of the mascarpone, the hazelnuts and a sprinkling of cinnamon.

The cakes will keep in an airtight container for up to 2 days, and without the topping can be frozen for up to 2 months.

note

To roast hazelnuts, spread them on a baking tray and bake in a preheated 200°C (400°F) oven for about 10 minutes, or until the skins start to split, checking now and then so they don't burn. Remove from the oven and leave to cool slightly. Tip the nuts into a tea towel (dish towel), rub the skins off and your nuts are ready to use.

apricot frangipane tart with ginger, orange & hazelnuts

This fruitful frangipane tart has a good zing from the orange, and a hint of warmth from the ground ginger. A base of almond meal keeps the tart lovely and moist, while also offering plenty of good fats and nutrients. You could use preserved or dried apricots here if you are unable to get fresh ones; just soften them in boiling water first.

SERVES 8 ◆ GF, VEG

100 g (3½ oz) butter
2 free-range eggs
175 g (6 oz/½ cup) honey
55 g (2 oz/⅓ cup) rice flour,
    45 g (1½ oz/⅓ cup) buckwheat
    flour or 40 g (1½ oz/⅓ cup)
    quinoa flour
100 g (3½ oz/1 cup) almond meal
zest of 1 lemon
½ teaspoon baking powder
5 fresh apricots, halved and pitted,
    or 10–12 dried apricots, soaked
    in water until soft and plump

Preheat the oven to 170°C (325°F). Grease a 25 cm (10 inch) tart (flan) tin.

Using an electric mixer, beat the butter in a bowl until pale. Gradually beat in the eggs one at a time, then the honey.

Gently fold in the flour, almond meal, lemon zest and baking powder. Pour the batter into the tart tin, then arrange the apricots around the top.

Bake for 30 minutes, or until a skewer inserted in the middle of the tart comes out clean.

Remove from the oven and leave in the tin until completely cool, before carefully turning out onto a plate. Cut into slices to serve.

The tart will keep for 2–3 days in an airtight container.

mandarin & poppy seed cakes
with coconut yoghurt

*Wonderfully moist, these boiled mandarin cakes are topped with coconut
yoghurt, and are naturally free of gluten, dairy and refined sugar.
Boiling the mandarins whole removes the bitterness from the skins and pith,
and gives the cakes a deliciously sweet and moist texture. I sometimes top them with
mascarpone cheese, which tastes spectacular also. Perfectly simple, sweet and elegant.*

MAKES 12 ◆ GF, DF (using coconut yoghurt), VEG

For the cakes
4 mandarins
200 g (7 oz/2 cups) almond meal
115 g (4 oz/⅓ cup) honey
4 free-range eggs
40 g (1½ oz/¼ cup) poppy seeds
1 teaspoon bicarbonate of soda
   (baking soda)
1 tablespoon apple cider vinegar

For the topping
125 g (4½ oz/½ cup) coconut
   yoghurt, plain yoghurt or
   mascarpone cheese
poppy seeds, for sprinkling

Place the whole mandarins in a large saucepan and cover with water.
Bring to the boil, then leave to boil for 1 hour. Drain, then allow to cool.

Meanwhile, preheat the oven to 160°C (315°F). Grease 12 holes of a
standard muffin tin.

Place the whole mandarins in a food processor — skin, pith, flesh and all!
Blitz until smooth. Add the remaining cake ingredients and blitz again
until smooth.

Pour the batter into the muffin holes and bake for 20–25 minutes, or until
a skewer inserted in the middle of a cake comes out clean. Remove from
the oven and allow to cool completely before removing from the tin.

To serve, turn the cooled cakes upside down, onto a plate. Top with a
generous smear of coconut yoghurt and a sprinkling of poppy seeds.

The cakes will keep for up to 3 days in an airtight container, and can be
frozen for up to 2 months.

luscious lemon, raspberry & honey bars

The shortbread-style crust in this luscious lemon slice is light yet slightly buttery in texture, and the topping creamy, tangy and not overly sweet. This slice keeps really well, so it's a great one to prepare ahead if you have a gathering of any kind coming up.

MAKES 8 ◆ GF, DF (using coconut oil), VEG

For the base

125 g (4½ oz/½ cup) coconut oil
   or butter, chilled
200 g (7 oz/2 cups) almond meal
80 g (2¾ oz/½ cup) rice flour
2 tablespoons honey
1 free-range egg

For the topping

125 ml (4 fl oz/½ cup) lemon juice
40 g (1½ oz/¼ cup) rice flour
4 free-range eggs
90 g (3¼ oz/¼ cup) honey
125 g (4½ oz/1 cup) raspberries
   (fresh or frozen)

Preheat the oven to 180°C (350°F). Find a slab tin measuring about 24 x 20 cm (9½ x 8 inches) and line it with baking paper.

Add all the base ingredients to a food processor and blend until the mixture starts to come together nicely. Press evenly into the tin, then prick with a fork four or five times.

Bake for 15–20 minutes, or until golden on top. Remove from the oven and leave to cool slightly while preparing the topping.

Reduce the oven temperature to 160°C (315°F).

Add all the topping ingredients, except the raspberries, to a blender or food processor. Whiz until smooth, then carefully pour the mixture over the slightly cooled base. Arrange the raspberries on top.

Bake for a further 30 minutes, or until the topping is cooked all the way through. Remove from the oven and leave to cool in the tin before slicing into bars.

The slice will keep for 3–4 days in an airtight container in the fridge.

peachy hand pies with a hint of ginger

If there's anything better than a large slice of comforting pie, it's a petite and buttery hand pie
that you can claim as your own and nibble with joy. Filled with sweet, sticky summer peaches,
these gorgeous little pies are crusty, flaky pockets of yumminess that can be eaten in three or four
good-sized bites — just the thing for summer picnics, or to slip into lunchboxes as a special treat.
I like to make up a double batch, then pop some of the finished pies into the freezer, so I can
simply thaw and bake a few at a time when in need of a sweet little treat.

MAKES 10   ◆   GF (if no spelt flour used), VEG

500 g (1 lb 2 oz) spelt flour
   or buckwheat flour, plus extra
   for dusting
50 g (1¾ oz/⅓ cup) coconut sugar,
   plus extra for dusting
350 g (12 oz) butter, chilled
   and cubed
1 teaspoon pure vanilla extract
zest and juice of 1 large lemon
3 large free-range eggs
milk, for brushing

For the filling
600 g (1 lb 5 oz) fresh peaches,
   peeled and diced; if not in
   season, use preserved or tinned
   ones and rinse off the syrup
1 teaspoon pure vanilla extract
juice of ½ lemon
2 tablespoons spelt, buckwheat
   or rice flour
½ teaspoon ground ginger
90 g (3¼ oz/¼ cup) honey, or
   60 ml (2 fl oz/¼ cup) maple
   syrup or brown rice syrup

Add the flour, coconut sugar, butter, vanilla and lemon zest and juice to a food processor. Add a pinch of sea salt and process until the mixture resembles dense breadcrumbs. Add the eggs and process until the mixture starts to come together like a dough.

Turn the dough out onto a floured surface. Knead lightly for 2–3 minutes. Shape into a ball, cover with plastic wrap and chill for 15–20 minutes.

Meanwhile, combine all the filling ingredients in a small bowl and stir well.

Line two baking trays with baking paper. Roll the dough out on a floured surface to about 5 mm (¼ inch) thick. Using a 10 cm (4 inch) round cookie cutter (or the rim of a glass), cut out as many circles as you can.

Transfer half the dough rounds to the baking trays, leaving 2 cm (¾ inch) between each. On each round, place about 2 tablespoons of the filling on the front edge of the circle, leaving about a 1 cm (½ inch) border.

Working with one round at a time, brush the edges with a little milk and pop a second circle on top. Use the tines of a fork to gently seal the edges. Repeat with the remaining dough circles.

Cut a few small slits in the top of each pie with a knife. Brush the tops with milk, and sprinkle with extra coconut sugar. Bake for 30 minutes, or until the tops begin to brown. Don't worry if some of the filling leaks out!

Remove from the oven and allow to cool for 10 minutes before eating.

The pies are best enjoyed the day they are made, but any leftovers will keep in a sealed container at room temperature for up to 1 week.

triple-chocolate truffles with pistachio

These deeply chocolatey truffles are ridiculously delicious, take about five minutes to make, and less than a minute to devour! We are all chocolate freaks in our family, and go crazy for these. Instead of cocoa nibs, you could roll the truffles in crushed nuts or seeds of your choice, although cocoa nibs enhance the chocolate effect. I dedicate these truffles to my beautiful sister Melanie, who is an absolute chocolate fiend.

MAKES ABOUT 20 ◆ GF, DF (if no butter used), VEG, V (using coconut oil)

For the truffles
100 g (3½ oz) good-quality
    dark chocolate
30 g (1 oz/¼ cup) good-quality
    unsweetened cocoa powder
160 g (5½ oz/1 cup) pitted
    medjool dates
100 g (3½ oz/1 cup) almond meal
50 g (1¾ oz/⅓ cup) rapadura,
    muscovado or coconut sugar
80 ml (2½ fl oz/⅓ cup) melted
    coconut oil or butter
75 g (2½ oz/½ cup) shelled
    pistachio nuts
zest and juice of 1 orange

For coating
70 g (2½ oz/½ cup) cocoa nibs

Add all the truffle ingredients, except the orange juice, to a food processor. Add a pinch of sea salt and process until the mixture resembles coarse crumbs. Add the orange juice and continue to process until the mixture starts to come together.

Using your hands, roll the mixture into small balls, then roll in the cocoa nibs until well coated.

Chill in the fridge for at least 30 minutes before serving.

The truffles will keep for up to 1 week in an airtight container in the fridge — if you can keep your hands off them that long.

FIG AND RAI...

Mash potato...
and juice. Beat...
1 hour. Bake or steam 1...

1lb. chopped figs
1lb. chopped raisins
1lb. bread crumbs
Milk
Vanilla

Stir all together to make a rather damp mixture...
Put into well buttered mould and steam 2 hours...
carefully, serve with sauce.

PRUNE AND FIG SHAPE

Line a buttered basin with soaked stoned prunes or figs split in
half, seeded side to mould. Soak 2ozs. stale bread crumbs in 1 pint
milk. Add 4ozs. raw sugar and 2 beaten eggs. Add this carefully
to mould. Tie over buttered paper and steam 1 hour.

RAISIN OR SULTANA PUDDING

1lb. each wholemeal flour,   1lb. seeded raisins
  butter and bread crumbs   Mixed peel to taste
1 egg   1 tablespoon raw sugar

Work butter into flour and crumbs, add fruit, etc., and egg last,
also a little milk. Steam 2 hours.

PATRICIA PUDDING

1lb. grated carrots   1lb. currants
1lb. granose flakes   ½ nutmeg

Teaspoon ground cloves, apple, banana, yolk of egg and a taste
prune juice.

PUDDING

2ozs. each raw sugar and
  cherries
½ teaspoon cinnamon

... enough ... Cream butter and sugar. Beat
crumb, carrot, yolk, cinnamon and cherries to
... egg white and steam 2½ hours in buttered

R APPLES

... whites and sweeten
... bake for 25 minutes.
... and serve with a

berry pinwheels with crème fraîche & coconut sugar

Sometimes life calls for something sweet, fruity and comforting. These berry pinwheels are just the thing. I've used spelt flour in these scones as I love its flavoursome character; it is also much easier on your digestion than regular flour. You could also use buckwheat flour if you would like them gluten free, although this will lend a strong earthiness to the scones.

MAKES 10–12 ◆ GF (using buckwheat flour), VEG

400 g (14 oz/4 cups) spelt flour, or 520 g (1 lb 2½ oz/4 cups) buckwheat flour, plus extra for dusting

1 tablespoon bicarbonate of soda (baking soda)

75 g (2½ oz/½ cup) coconut sugar

½ teaspoon sea salt

220 g (7¾ oz/1 cup) crème fraîche; if unavailable, use sour cream or yoghurt instead

2 teaspoons pure vanilla extract

4 free-range eggs

350 g (12 oz) unsalted butter, frozen or well chilled

150 g (5½ oz/1½ cups) blackberry chia jam (see Note on page 94), or 185 g (6½ oz/1½ cups) fresh blackberries

To finish
1 free-range egg, lightly beaten
coconut sugar, for sprinkling

Preheat the oven to 200°C (400°F). Line a baking tray with baking paper.

Mix the flour, bicarbonate of soda, coconut sugar and sea salt together in a large bowl.

In a separate bowl, whisk together the crème fraîche, vanilla and eggs.

Coarsely grate the frozen butter, then add it to the flour mixture. Toss with your fingers until the butter is evenly coated.

Add the crème fraîche mixture to the flour mixture and fold with a spatula until just combined.

Transfer the dough to a floured surface. Dust the top with extra flour. Now knead the dough six to eight times, until it resembles a ragged ball, adding more flour if it is sticking too much.

Using a floured rolling pin, roll the dough into a large square about 1 cm (½ inch) thick. Spread the blackberry jam evenly over the dough, or scatter the blackberries over, then roll up carefully into a log.

Slice into pinwheels about 3 cm (1¼ inches) thick and place on the baking tray. Brush the tops with the beaten egg, then sprinkle generously with coconut sugar.

Bake for 15–20 minutes, or until slightly golden on top. Transfer to a wire rack and leave to cool for 10 minutes before serving.

These pinwheels are best served warm.

hummingbird pineapple cake
with mascarpone frosting

*A more wholesome take on the classic hummingbird cake, this recipe
includes fresh pineapple, with a little coconut oil for a slightly tropical
flavour. Filled with currants and almonds, this moist and fruity cake
will be a favourite for years to come.*

SERVES 8 ◆ GF, VEG

zest and juice of 2 oranges

260 g (9¼ oz/1 cup) tinned crushed
pineapple, drained well (or use
the same quantity of fresh
pineapple, finely chopped)

1 tablespoon apple cider vinegar

80 ml (2½ oz/⅓ cup) melted
coconut oil

4 free-range eggs

115 g (4 oz/⅓ cup) honey

250 g (9 oz/2½ cups) almond meal

110 g (3¾ oz/¾ cup) currants

1 teaspoon ground cinnamon

1 teaspoon bicarbonate of soda
(baking soda)

For the mascarpone topping

220 g (7¾ oz/1 cup) mascarpone
cheese

juice and zest of 1 lemon

2 tablespoons honey

a handful of silvered almonds

Preheat the oven to 160°C (315°F). Grease a 22 cm (8½ inch) cake tin.

Add the orange zest, orange juice, pineapple, vinegar, melted coconut
oil, eggs and honey to a food processor and blend until smooth.

Add the almond meal, currants, cinnamon and bicarbonate of soda
and continue to process until combined.

Pour the batter into the cake tin and bake for 40–45 minutes, or until
a skewer inserted in the middle comes out clean.

Remove from the oven and leave to cool completely in the tin, before
carefully transferring to a plate.

To make the topping, combine the mascarpone, lemon zest, lemon
juice and honey in a bowl. Mix until well combined. Spread evenly over
the top of the cake, then sprinkle with the almonds.

The cake will keep in an airtight container in the fridge for up to 3 days.
Without the topping, the cake can be frozen for up to 1 month.

THE
DINNER
TABLE

When I wake in the morning, one of the first thoughts that runs through my mind is what I'll be preparing for dinner that evening.

I am hopelessly in love with every aspect of food — where it comes from, how it is grown, its health benefits, and how to make it taste unbelievably delicious. It is this obsession that inspires me to spend hours on end in the kitchen, conjuring up these wonderful creations to share with you.

In this chapter, I have mostly taken classic family favourites and added a wholesome twist. As you have probably already noticed, I like to keep it really simple, using plenty of herbs and aromatic flavours in scrumptious combinations.

Whether you are in the mood for something quick and easy, light and delicate, or hearty and comforting, I am positive you will find something in here to tickle your fancy.

garlic, sage & cauliflower risotto

*Garlic, sage and butter are such a gorgeous combination, and they really
shine in this amazingly oozy and creamy risotto. If someone made me
this for dinner, I would be one very happy lady.*

SERVES 6 ◆ GF, VEG

2 tablespoons butter, ghee or
olive oil
1 large leek, pale part only, halved
lengthways, then thinly sliced
6 garlic cloves, roughly chopped
a large handful of fresh sage
leaves, roughly chopped
500 g (1 lb 2 oz/2¼ cups) arborio
or other risotto rice
2 glasses white wine
1.5 litres (52 fl oz/6 cups)
good-quality chicken stock
½ head of cauliflower, cut into
florets

To serve
40 g (1½ oz) butter
100 g (3½ oz/1 cup) grated
parmesan cheese
herbs or salad greens, to garnish

Melt the butter in a large heavy-based saucepan over medium heat.
Add the leek, garlic and sage. Cook, stirring, for about 5 minutes, until
the leek has softened and is slightly browned.

Add the rice and lightly fry for a couple of minutes, stirring to stop the rice
burning. Pour in the wine and continue to cook for a few more minutes,
until the wine has been absorbed into the rice.

Add a ladleful of stock, along with the cauliflower, and turn the heat down
to low. Simmer gently for a minute or so, until the rice has fully absorbed
the liquid. Continue to add the remaining stock one ladleful at a time,
stirring to massage the creamy starch out of the rice.

Once all the stock has been added, taste to see if the rice is cooked; it
should take about 20 minutes all up. The rice should be soft, but with a
subtle bite. If not, add a little water and continue to cook and stir until
perfectly done.

Season to taste with sea salt and freshly ground black pepper. Remove
from the heat and gently stir in the butter and parmesan. Place a lid on
top and leave to sit for 1–2 minutes before serving, garnished with herbs.

potato bake with rosemary & cheddar

We love this warming winter potato bake, layered with sharp vintage cheddar cheese. It is topped with one of my favourite herbs, aromatic and earthy rosemary, which goes gorgeously crisp in the oven. This is one of those dishes that tastes even better the next day. It also makes a scrumptious breakfast served with poached eggs and wilted English spinach; I like to add a little more cheese, and a good drizzle of olive oil, then grill it in a hot pan.

SERVES 5–6 AS A SIDE OR LIGHT MEAL   ◆   GF, VEG

6–8 large roasting potatoes; agria work well
250 g (9 oz/2 cups) grated cheddar cheese
8 free-range eggs
60 ml (2 fl oz/¼ cup) milk
a large handful of fresh rosemary leaves
a drizzle of extra virgin olive oil

Preheat the oven to 180°C (350°F).

Scrub the potatoes, then slice into rounds about 1 cm (½ inch) thick. Place in a saucepan of salted water and bring to the boil. Reduce the heat to low and simmer for 2–3 minutes. Drain the water, then immediately fill the pan with cold water to stop the potato cooking any further.

Once the potato slices have cooled, arrange a layer of them in a baking dish, completely covering the bottom. Sprinkle with a small handful of the cheese, then repeat two or three times until you have used all the potato slices, reserving a little cheese for topping.

In a bowl, whisk together the eggs, milk and a large pinch of sea salt and freshly ground black pepper. Pour the egg mixture on top of the potato slices. Sprinkle with the rosemary, then drizzle with a little olive oil.

Bake for 35–40 minutes, or until the potato is tender and the cheese is golden brown. Serve warm.

jamaican jerk chicken

*In this fabulously fragrant dish, chicken breasts are marinated in a punchy
Caribbean-style sauce full of warm, delicious spices. We grill the chicken on
the barbecue to intensify the flavours, but you can also cook it in a frying pan.
For maximum flavour, I recommend letting the chicken marinate overnight.*

SERVES 8; THIS RECIPE CAN EASILY BE HALVED ◆ GF, DF (IF SERVING WITHOUT YOGHURT)

8 skinless chicken breast fillets

For the marinade

4 large garlic cloves, peeled

2 tablespoons chilli flakes

1 red onion, chopped

35 g (1¼ oz/¼ cup) coconut
   or muscovado sugar

a large handful of fresh
   thyme sprigs

2 tablespoons ground allspice

1 tablespoon sea salt

1 teaspoon ground nutmeg

1 teaspoon ground cinnamon

125 ml (4 fl oz/½ cup) apple
   cider vinegar

60 ml (2 fl oz/¼ cup) soy sauce

60 ml (2 fl oz/¼ cup) freshly
   squeezed lime juice

60 ml (2 fl oz/¼ cup) freshly
   squeezed orange juice

60 ml (2 fl oz/¼ cup) olive oil

1 teaspoon freshly ground
   black pepper

To serve

coriander (cilantro) sprigs

2 limes, quartered

garden greens

250 g (9 oz/1 cup) plain yoghurt

Add the marinade ingredients to a blender or food processor and blend
until smooth.

Lay the chicken breasts in a large container or baking dish. Pour the
marinade over and gently toss together, making sure the marinade coats
the chicken well. Cover and leave to marinate in the fridge for at least
3–4 hours, or preferably overnight.

Grill the chicken breasts on a hot barbecue, chargrill pan or in a frying pan
over medium–high heat for 4–5 minutes on each side, or until the juices
run clear when a skewer is inserted into the thickest part of the chicken.

Carve the chicken into slices about 1 cm (½ inch) thick. Serve warm,
garnished with coriander, with garden greens and lime wedges on the
side, and some plain yoghurt for dolloping over.

the best roast chicken with fennel salt & crispy smashed potatoes

This is one of those brilliantly comforting meals that's just perfect for a lazy Sunday. The roast chicken is juicy, tender and delicately fragrant from the fennel seeds. The crispy potatoes are roasted in the same dish and soak up all the delicious juices; the trick is to smash them just before serving, using a potato masher. This really gets the flavours going — they just seem to melt and mingle into each other. A true delight.

SERVES 4 ◆ GF, DF (if no ghee or butter used)

2 tablespoons fennel seeds
2 tablespoons sea salt
1 brown onion, roughly chopped
2 celery stalks, roughly chopped
6 roasting potatoes, scrubbed and
  cut into quarters
2 lemons
1 garlic bulb, each clove smashed
  (no need to peel them first)
500 ml (17 fl oz/2 cups)
  good-quality chicken stock
2 tablespoons olive oil, for drizzling
1.5 kg (3 lb 5 oz) whole free-range
  chicken
2–3 tablespoons melted ghee,
  butter or olive oil
a handful of mixed fresh thyme,
  rosemary and sage leaves
extra virgin olive oil, for drizzling
a large handful of roughly chopped
  flat-leaf (Italian) parsley

Preheat the oven to 180°C (350°F).

Using a mortar and pestle, bash the fennel seeds and sea salt together until finely ground.

Arrange the onion, celery and potatoes in a large baking dish. Cut one of the lemons into quarters and add to the baking dish, along with the garlic. Pour the stock over the top, then drizzle generously with olive oil.

Lay the chicken on top, and place the remaining lemon inside the cavity. Rub the melted ghee into the skin, then sprinkle with the fennel salt and some freshly ground black pepper. Lastly, scatter the thyme, rosemary and sage on top.

Bake for 1½ hours, basting the chicken halfway through. Check the chicken is cooked by piercing the thigh with a skewer; the juices should run clear.

Transfer the chicken to a board to rest for 10 minutes or so before carving.

Using a potato masher, gently smash the potatoes. Drizzle with extra virgin olive oil, scatter the parsley over and serve with the chicken.

zucchini bake with feta & sage

When I'm working from home, I quite often make this zucchini bake, topped with crispy, aromatic sage and salty feta cheese. This light meal celebrates all that is fantastic about the beautiful egg, and is wonderfully simple to prepare. We simply serve it with salad greens tossed in olive oil, lemon juice and a little sea salt. The leftovers also make a quick nutritious dinner, which the kids really love.

SERVES 6 ◆ VEG

8 free-range eggs
25 g (1 oz/¼ cup) spelt flour
(see note)
8 zucchini (courgettes), sliced into
rounds 1 cm (½ inch) thick
a handful of fresh sage leaves
75 g (2½ oz/½ cup) crumbled
feta cheese

Preheat the oven to 180°C (350°F). Grease a 20 x 24 cm (8 x 9½ inch) baking dish or line it with baking paper.

Add the eggs, flour and a good pinch of sea salt and freshly ground black pepper to a blender and whiz until smooth; alternatively you could whisk the eggs in a bowl.

Layer the zucchini slices in the baking dish, then pour the egg mixture over the top. Scatter the sage and feta over.

Bake for 30 minutes, or until the zucchini is tender and cooked through.

note ◇◇◇◇◇◇◇◇◇◇◇◇◇◇◇◇◇◇◇◇◇◇◇◇◇◇◇◇◇◇◇◇◇◇◇◇

Instead of spelt flour, you could use quinoa, rice or buckwheat flour to make this slice gluten free.

wonderful french onion soup

To me, onion soup is the perfect autumn affair. Its delicious depth of flavour warms me right to the core. The slow-cooked caramelised onions have the most wonderful sweetness that partners perfectly with the woody thyme undertones. While simmering away on the stove, it gives off the most beautiful sweet herby aroma. The ultimate autumn comfort.

SERVES 4 ◆ GF, DF (if no ghee, butter or cream used), VEG, V (if no ghee, butter or cream used)

2 tablespoons ghee, butter or
olive oil
6 onions, cut in half, then roughly
chopped
1 garlic bulb, each clove peeled
and roughly chopped
a handful of fresh thyme sprigs,
roughly chopped
2 tablespoons honey
1 litre (35 fl oz/4 cups) good-quality
vegetable stock
cream, to serve (optional)

In a large saucepan, melt the ghee over medium heat until sizzling. Add the onion, garlic and thyme. Sauté for about 5 minutes, or until the onion is soft, then drizzle in the honey.

Turn the heat down to low and continue to stir every so often until the onion turns a lovely dark caramel colour; this can take 20–30 minutes. If the onion starts to stick to the bottom of the pan, stir in a little water. Do not try to rush the caramelisation process, as it is time that builds a lovely depth of flavour.

Add the stock, 500 ml (17 fl oz/2 cups) water and a generous pinch of sea salt and freshly ground black pepper. Bring to the boil, then simmer on low for a further 35–45 minutes, or until the soup has reduced by half.

Serve with a dollop of cream if desired, and a sprinkling of black pepper.

roasted red capsicum soup

*This is an astonishingly beautiful soup of roasted red capsicums, enhanced
with thyme and a dash of crème fraîche. It has the most lovely hint
of sweetness, and a touch of earthiness from the herbs.*

SERVES 4 ◆ GF, DF (if no ghee, butter, crème fraîche or sour cream used),
VEG, V (using vegetable stock and no ghee, butter, crème fraîche or sour cream)

4 large red capsicums (peppers)
125 ml (4 fl oz/½ cup) melted ghee,
    butter or olive oil
6 garlic cloves, roughly chopped
1 onion, diced
a small handful of fresh thyme
    leaves, roughly chopped
2 carrots, roughly chopped
1 celery stalk, roughly chopped
1 bay leaf
1 litre (35 fl oz/4 cups) good-quality
    chicken or vegetable stock
60 g (2¼ oz/¼ cup) crème fraîche
    or sour cream (optional)

Preheat the oven to 200°C (400°F). Place a wire rack towards the top
of the oven.

Place the whole capsicums in a baking dish. Using a pastry brush, lightly
coat them with some of the melted ghee, reserving the left-over ghee.

Roast the capsicums for 15 minutes, or until blackened on top. Flip each
capsicum over, then roast for another 15 minutes, or until the other side
is also soft and blackened. Remove from the oven and leave until cool
enough to handle

Using your hands, remove the stems, seeds and the charred skin from
the capsicums, then set the flesh aside.

Add the remaining melted ghee to a large soup pot and place over
medium heat. Sauté the garlic, onion and thyme for about 5 minutes,
or until the onion is soft. Add the carrot and celery and continue to
cook, stirring, for another 5 minutes or so.

Add the capsicum flesh, bay leaf and stock and bring to a soft boil.
Reduce the heat to low and simmer for 25 minutes.

Leave the soup to cool slightly, then add the crème fraîche, if using. Blend
until smooth, using a hand-held stick blender, or in batches in an upright
blender. Season to taste with sea salt and freshly ground black pepper.

Gently reheat for serving; any left-over soup will keep for 4 days in the
fridge, or up to 3 months in an airtight container in the freezer.

baked ratatouille with olives & parmesan

Fantastically comforting, this ratatouille is full of gorgeous melt-in-your-mouth Mediterranean vegetables: red capsicums, eggplant, juicy ripe tomatoes and a splash of red wine vinegar to really intensify the flavours. I sometimes serve this as a stand-alone dinner, with a simple salad, although it also makes a wonderful vegetable side dish.

SERVES 4 ◆ GF, VEG

3 tablespoons ghee, butter or
  olive oil
2 red onions, diced
1 garlic bulb, peeled and roughly
  chopped
a large handful of fresh thyme
  leaves, roughly chopped
2 eggplants (aubergines), diced
2 red capsicums (peppers), diced
2 zucchini (courgettes), diced
5 large tomatoes, roughly chopped;
  alternatively, you could use
  2 x 400 g (14 oz) tins chopped
  tomatoes
2 tablespoons good-quality
  red wine vinegar
500 ml (17 fl oz/2 cups)
  good-quality vegetable stock

For topping
175 g (6 oz/1 cup) green olives,
  pitted
2 large handfuls of shaved
  parmesan cheese
a large handful of pepitas
  (pumpkin seeds) and sunflower
  seeds (optional)

Preheat the oven to 180°C (350°F).

Melt the ghee in a large heavy-based saucepan. Add the onion, garlic and thyme and sauté for about 5 minutes, or until the onion is soft. Add the eggplant, capsicum and zucchini and cook for a further 5 minutes, stirring occasionally.

Stir in the tomatoes and vinegar and cook for 2–3 minutes, then pour in the stock. Turn the heat down to low and simmer for about 10 minutes, until almost all the liquid has evaporated. Season to taste with sea salt and freshly ground black pepper.

Transfer the mixture to a baking dish, then top with the olives, parmesan and seeds, if using. Bake for 25–30 minutes, or until golden on top and bubbling around the edges. Serve hot.

pumpkin, oregano & garlic soup
with crispy bacon crumbs

This golden, velvety pumpkin soup is wonderfully nourishing and heartwarming. Roughly torn oregano gives a fantastic fragrant and earthy touch, and the garlic at the end adds a lovely kick. Topped with thick, creamy yoghurt and a generous sprinkle of deliciously crispy, salty bacon crumbs, it is perfection in a bowl.

SERVES 6   ◆   GF, DF (using olive oil and no yoghurt, sour cream or crème fraîche)

1 pumpkin (winter squash), peeled and chopped into thick pieces

1.5–2 litres (52–70 fl oz/6–8 cups) good-quality vegetable or chicken stock

2 tablespoons ghee, butter or extra virgin olive oil

2 garlic cloves, peeled

To serve

6 free-range bacon rashers, rind removed

4 large tablespoons Greek-style yoghurt, sour cream or crème fraîche

a large handful of fresh oregano leaves, roughly chopped

extra virgin olive oil, for drizzling

Put the pumpkin in a stockpot or large saucepan and cover with the stock. Bring to a gentle boil, then reduce the heat to a simmer and cook for 30 minutes, or until the pumpkin is tender and the liquid has reduced slightly.

Leave to cool for 5 minutes, then transfer to a blender, one ladleful at a time. Add the ghee and garlic cloves and blend until smooth. Season to taste with sea salt and freshly ground black pepper.

Grill, fry or bake the bacon until crispy, then roughly chop into crumb-sized pieces.

Gently reheat the soup and ladle into bowls. Top with a dollop of yoghurt, then the bacon crumbs. Sprinkle with the oregano and some extra pepper. Drizzle with olive oil and serve.

slow-cooked lamb shanks with cinnamon & orange zest

Long, gentle cooking renders these aromatic lamb shanks lusciously tender and rich — slightly sweet, with a subtle hum of cinnamon, and a kick of citrus. We find this dish doesn't need any accompaniments, as the lentils beef the dish up quite a bit.

SERVES 4 ◆ GF, DF (if no butter used)

40 g (1½ oz) butter (or use 2 tablespoons olive oil if you'd like to be dairy free)
2–3 onions, finely chopped
2 carrots, grated
4 garlic cloves, finely chopped
juice and zest of 1 orange
2 tablespoons honey
a thumb-sized piece of fresh ginger, peeled and grated
2 tablespoons tomato paste (concentrated purée)
4 lamb shanks
2 teaspoons ground cinnamon
1 litre (35 fl oz/4 cups) good-quality beef stock
a handful of fresh rosemary leaves; sage or thyme also work well
a handful of flat-leaf (Italian) parsley, plus extra to serve
400 g (14 oz) tin lentils, rinsed and drained
juice of 1 lemon

Preheat the oven to 180°C (350°F).

In a frying pan over medium heat, melt half the butter until sizzling. Add the onion and sauté for about 5 minutes, or until soft and translucent. Transfer to a large casserole dish with a lid.

Add the carrot, garlic, orange zest, orange juice, honey, ginger and tomato paste to the casserole dish and set aside.

Heat the remaining butter in the same frying pan, over medium heat. Brown the lamb shanks on all sides; you may need to do this in batches so as not to overcrowd the pan.

Transfer the shanks to the casserole dish, then sprinkle with the cinnamon and a generous pinch of sea salt and freshly ground black pepper. Pour in the stock, adding a little water if necessary to cover the shanks, then top with the herbs. Put the lid on and bake for 2 hours.

Remove from the oven and stir in the lentils. Bake for a further 1 hour, or until the meat is super tender and falling off the bone.

Finish with an extra sprinkling of parsley, and a squeeze of lemon juice. Serve straight away.

summer soup with lettuce, leek, peas & mint

A simple, honest and calming soup with light, delicate flavours, and a lovely nutty, chewy texture from the buckwheat. In the colder months, you could make this soup with dark leafy greens instead of lettuce, and use earthier herbs such as thyme or oregano.

SERVES 4–6 ◆ GF (if served with GF bread), DF (if no ghee or butter used), VEG (using vegetable stock), V (using vegetable stock and no ghee or butter)

2 tablespoons ghee, butter
    or olive oil
2 leeks, pale part only, sliced
    lengthways, then thinly sliced
2 celery stalks, thinly sliced
220 g (7¾ oz/1 cup) buckwheat
    groats, rinsed well
½ iceberg or cos (romaine) lettuce,
    thinly sliced
155 g (5½ oz/1 cup) fresh or
    frozen peas
2 litres (70 fl oz/8 cups)
    good-quality vegetable or
    chicken stock
a large handful of mint leaves,
    roughly chopped
juice of 1 lemon

To serve
chopped flat-leaf (Italian) parsley,
    for sprinkling
crusty sourdough or gluten-free
    bread

Heat the ghee in a stockpot or large saucepan over medium heat. Add the leek and celery and cook, stirring occasionally, for 5 minutes, or until softened.

Add the buckwheat, lettuce and peas, then pour in the stock. Bring to a soft boil, then leave to simmer for 20 minutes, or until the buckwheat is nice and soft.

Stir in the mint and lemon juice. Season to taste with sea salt and freshly ground black pepper.

Serve with a sprinkling of parsley, and crusty bread of your choice.

lentil lasagne with rainbow chard & buffalo feta

Packed full of vegetables, this wholesome lasagne can be made using whatever fresh produce you happen to have on hand. This version uses rainbow chard (a vibrantly coloured variety of silverbeet) and sweet potato instead of pasta sheets, and a rich tomato lentil filling instead of minced (ground) beef. Trust me, your meat-loving friends won't even notice the difference!

SERVES 4 GENEROUSLY ◆ GF, VEG

6 large sweet potatoes, peeled and very thinly sliced

6 rainbow chard leaves, stems removed; you could also use silverbeet (Swiss chard), English spinach or kale

100 g (3½ oz) buffalo feta cheese, crumbled

For the lentil filling

2 x 400 g (14 oz) tins lentils, rinsed and drained

400 g (14 oz) tin chopped tomatoes

125 g (4½ oz/½ cup) tomato paste (concentrated purée)

60 ml (2 fl oz/¼ cup) olive oil

For the béchamel sauce

40 g (1½ oz) butter

2 tablespoons rice flour, cornflour (cornstarch) or potato flour

250 ml (9 fl oz/1 cup) full-cream (whole) organic milk

a large handful of fresh herbs, such as parsley, chives and basil, roughly chopped

¼ teaspoon ground nutmeg

Preheat the oven to 180°C (350°F). Grease a 30 x 35 cm (12 x 14 inch) baking dish.

Put all the lentil filling ingredients in a bowl. Season with a good pinch of sea salt and freshly ground black pepper, mix well and set aside.

To make the béchamel sauce, melt the butter in a saucepan over medium heat. Stir in the rice flour until smooth, then cook for 1–2 minutes, until bubbling and golden brown. Pour in the milk and whisk well until smooth. Add the herbs, nutmeg and a pinch of salt and pepper. Continue to whisk for about 5 minutes, until the sauce thickens. Remove from the heat.

To assemble the lasagne, first add a layer of sweet potato to the baking dish, then a layer of chard. Top with the lentil sauce, then layer again with the sweet potato and chard.

Pour the béchamel sauce over the lasagne, then sprinkle the crumbled feta over the top.

Bake for 45 minutes, or until golden on top and bubbling around the edges. Leave to cool slightly before serving.

beef schnitzels with a crispy seed crumb

My readers often ask me for simple, finger food dinner ideas that kids will enjoy — this one certainly fits the bill. My two little ones love these crispy seed-crumbed schnitzels, and even enjoy helping prepare them. We like ours served with Home-made tomato sauce (see page 70) and a delicious selection of cherry tomatoes, cucumber and baby carrots.

SERVES 4 ◆ GF, DF

500 g (1 lb 2 oz) thin-cut
   minute steaks
2 free-range eggs
olive oil, for pan-frying
Home-made tomato sauce
   (see page 70), to serve

For the seed crumbs
40 g (1½ oz/¼ cup) sesame seeds
40 g (1½ oz/¼ cup) pepitas
   (pumpkin seeds)
30 g (1 oz/¼ cup) sunflower seeds
2 garlic cloves, crushed
2 tablespoons dried rosemary
   or oregano
1 tablespoon sea salt
1 teaspoon freshly ground
   black pepper

Using a meat tenderiser, pound each steak three or four times on both sides. This will help break down the muscle fibres and tenderise the meat.

Whisk the eggs in a shallow bowl, then set aside. In a separate shallow bowl, combine all the seed crumb ingredients.

Dip each steak in the beaten egg, then in the seed crumb mix.

Heat a little olive oil in a large frying pan over medium heat. Cook the schnitzels for 3–4 minutes on each side, or until the crumbs are golden and crispy.

Serve warm, cut into smaller portions if desired, with a small bowl of the tomato sauce.

tomato-braised chicken with anchovies, rosemary & garlic

Something amazing happens when you roast chicken, anchovies and garlic together. The flavours seem to melt into one another, and really make this dish sing. This version simply uses tinned tomatoes, although it would be great to use ripe, juicy tomatoes when they are in season. We serve this dish with cooked white rice or buttery mashed root vegetables.

SERVES 4 ◆ GF, DF

8 free-range chicken drumsticks
2 x 400 g (14 oz) tins chopped
   tomatoes, or about 750 g
   (1 lb 10 oz/3 cups) chopped
   fresh tomatoes
extra virgin olive oil, for drizzling
85 g (3 oz) jar of anchovies,
   drained
a handful of fresh rosemary sprigs

Preheat the oven to 180°C (350°F).

Arrange the chicken drumsticks in a large baking dish, then top with the tomatoes. Drizzle generously with olive oil and sprinkle with sea salt and freshly ground black pepper. Lay the anchovies on top, then scatter the rosemary over.

Bake for 1 hour, or until the chicken is tender and cooked through.

massaged kale salad with toasted pecans, ricotta & chilli vinaigrette

With a fabulous hint of garlic and chilli, and topped with creamy ricotta
and toasted pecans, this wintry salad is kicking with flavour. It is beautiful
on its own, or served with grilled meat or fish.

SERVES 4–5 ◆ GF, VEG

100 g (3½ oz/1 cup) pecans
6 kale leaves, stems removed,
    leaves thinly sliced
1 head of broccoli, cut into very
    thin florets
350 g (12 oz/2 cups) cooked
    chickpeas, drained and rinsed
250 g (9 oz/1 cup) fresh ricotta
    cheese

For the chilli vinaigrette
80 ml (2½ fl oz/⅓ cup) extra virgin
    olive oil
juice of 2 lemons
1 garlic clove, thinly sliced
a pinch of chilli flakes
½ teaspoon sea salt
a good pinch of freshly ground
    black pepper

Put the pecans in a small frying pan without any oil. Fry over medium heat for 2–3 minutes, or until fragrant and toasty. Tip onto a chopping board and allow to cool slightly, then crush with a rolling pin and set aside.

In a small bowl, whisk all the vinaigrette ingredients until well combined.

Add the kale to a large bowl, then drizzle the vinaigrette all over. Gently massage the vinaigrette into the kale leaves with your hands. Add the broccoli and chickpeas, then toss well.

Divide the salad among serving bowls, then top with large chunks of ricotta. Sprinkle with the crushed pecans and serve.

chickpeas braised in a rich sun-dried tomato & oregano sauce

Here's some nourishing inspiration for a cold winter's day. This is one of those fabulous dishes that uses mostly pantry ingredients — perfect if you haven't been to the shops for a little while. It has the warmth and comfort of a soup, but is a little heartier. I like to make up a double batch, in my largest cast-iron pot, as these warming chickpeas make a gorgeous quick lunch or dinner, topped with a poached egg and a sprinkling of toasted pepitas. A real winner.

SERVES 4–6 ◆ GF, DF (if no ghee or butter used), VEG (using vegetable stock)

3 tablespoons ghee, butter or
    olive oil
2 brown onions, diced
6–8 garlic cloves, roughly chopped
150 g (5½ oz/1 cup) sun-dried
    tomatoes, roughly chopped
a large handful of fresh oregano
    leaves, roughly chopped
1 tablespoon honey
1 glass white wine (optional)
4 potatoes, peeled and cut into
    small cubes
500 ml (17 fl oz/2 cups)
    good-quality vegetable or
    chicken stock
2 x 400 g (14 oz) tins chopped
    tomatoes
2 x 400 g (14 oz) tins chickpeas,
    rinsed and drained
4–6 soft-poached eggs, to serve
    (optional)
pepitas (pumpkin seeds),
    for sprinkling

Melt the ghee in a large heavy-based saucepan over medium heat. Add the onion, garlic, sun-dried tomatoes, oregano and honey. Sauté for 10–12 minutes, or until the onion is soft and slightly browned.

Add the wine, if using, and cook, stirring, for a further 5 minutes. Add the potato, stock, tinned tomatoes and chickpeas and bring to a soft boil. Reduce the heat to low and simmer for 45 minutes, stirring every now and then, until the sauce is thick and pulpy.

Season to taste with sea salt and freshly ground black pepper. Serve topped with a poached egg if desired, and a sprinkling of pepitas.

slow-braised capsicum with balsamic vinegar & mint

Perfectly tender and full of gorgeous flavour, here is my version of a pepperonata, slowly braised with balsamic vinegar and mint. It is wonderful spooned over a buttery cauliflower mash and served with pan-fried fish.

SERVES 4–6 ◆ GF, DF, VEG, V

extra virgin olive oil, for pan-frying
4 red capsicums (peppers), cut into
  strips about 1 cm (½ inch) thick
60 ml (2 fl oz/¼ cup) balsamic
  vinegar
a large handful of mint leaves,
  roughly chopped

Add enough olive oil to a cast-iron saucepan or large heavy-based frying pan to cover the bottom of the pan. Warm the oil over medium heat.

Add the capsicum strips, stirring to coat them in the oil. Cover the pan, then reduce the heat to very low. Cook for 20–25 minutes, stirring every now and then, until the capsicum has softened.

Remove from the heat and add the vinegar and mint. Season with a good pinch of sea salt and freshly ground black pepper and stir until combined.

Serve warm, or cover and refrigerate until required. The dish will keep in the fridge for several days; bring back to room temperature for serving.

creamy garlic & thyme chicken
with cauliflower couscous

You will love this one! I've been making this dish for my husband for the last three years. It's his favourite and, if I am being honest, it's pretty damn delicious. The chicken is rich, tender and full of flavour, served with a light, herby cauliflower couscous for mopping up all the creamy sauce. A beautiful dish, bound to give you great happiness.

SERVES 4 ◆ GF

40 g (1½ oz) butter

4 garlic cloves, roughly chopped

1 brown onion, diced

500 g (1 lb 2 oz) free-range skinless chicken breast fillets, cut into bite-sized pieces

a handful of fresh thyme leaves, finely chopped

250 ml (9 fl oz/1 cup) white wine (optional)

250 ml (9 fl oz/1 cup) good-quality chicken stock

250 ml (9 fl oz/1 cup) thin (pouring/whipping) cream

juice of ½ lemon

For the cauliflower couscous

1 cauliflower, broken into florets

a large handful of flat-leaf (Italian) parsley, finely chopped

juice of 1 lemon

60 ml (2 fl oz/¼ cup) extra virgin olive oil

In a large frying pan over medium heat, melt the butter until sizzling. Add the garlic and onion and sauté for about 10 minutes, or until the onion is translucent.

Add the chicken, thyme and a pinch of freshly ground black pepper, then continue to cook until the chicken is browned all over.

Stir in the wine, if using, and simmer until all the liquid has evaporated. Pour in the stock, then turn the heat down to low and cook for about 15–20 minutes.

Meanwhile, prepare the cauliflower couscous. Place the cauliflower in a food processor and pulse to a rice-like consistency. Transfer to a heatproof bowl, cover with boiling water and leave to blanch for 1 minute. Drain immediately.

Toss the cauliflower in a bowl with the parsley, lemon juice, olive oil and a pinch of sea salt and freshly ground black pepper. Set aside until ready to serve.

Continue to cook the chicken until all the stock has simmered off. Finally, stir in the cream and bring to a soft boil.

Remove from the heat, then stir the lemon juice through. Serve with the cauliflower couscous.

root vegetable
roast with melting
goat's feta

◇◇◇◇◇◇◇◇◇

recipe page 190

root vegetable roast
with melting goat's feta

A simple dish celebrating root vegetables and their earthy goodness. All you need to do is just place everything in one roasting dish — no fluffing around at all. This roasted vegetable medley is delicious on its own, or great served alongside a roast. For a dairy-free or vegan option, simply leave out the cheese.

SERVES 4 ◆ GF, VEG

8 baby carrots
2 beetroot (beets), peeled
   and diced
2 potatoes, peeled and diced
2 orange sweet potatoes, peeled
   and diced
2 red onions, roughly chopped
1 garlic bulb, each clove peeled
   and smashed
a handful of fresh oregano sprigs
100 g (3½ oz) goat's feta (or cow's
   feta, if unavailable)
80 ml (2½ fl oz/⅓ cup) extra virgin
   olive oil
juice of 1 lemon

Preheat the oven to 180°C (350°F).

Arrange all the vegetables and garlic in a large baking dish. Sprinkle with the oregano, then scatter the feta over the top. Drizzle with the olive oil and lemon juice, then season generously with sea salt and freshly ground black pepper.

Bake for 40–45 minutes, or until the vegetables are tender and slightly crisp around the edges. Serve hot.

Recipe photograph on page 188

baked salmon parcels with a herb & lemon zest butter

This is one of my favourite ways to cook fish. Baking the salmon in parcels keeps in all the moisture and allows the gorgeous flavours and juices to mingle. It is wonderful with the Petite potato salad (see page 114) and a fresh green salad for a quick, easy supper.

SERVES 4–6 ◆ GF

4 salmon fillets, sliced in half
2 lemons, each sliced into 4 rounds

For the herb butter
250 g (9 oz) organic butter,
　　at room temperature
a handful of fresh thyme, parsley
　　or oregano leaves, thinly sliced
zest of 1 large lemon

Combine the herb butter ingredients in a small bowl. Using the back of a spoon, mix until soft and creamy.

Spoon the butter onto a 30 cm (12 inch) square of baking paper. Roll the paper up into a round bon bon or Christmas-cracker shape, and twist the ends to secure. Pop into the fridge or freezer for about 30 minutes to set.

Meanwhile, preheat the oven to 180°C (350°F).

To prepare the salmon parcels, cut out eight squares of baking paper, each about 25 cm (10 inches) wide. Have some kitchen twine ready for tying up the parcels.

Place a piece of salmon on each piece of baking paper. Top each piece with a slice of lemon.

Remove the herb butter from the fridge or freezer, and cut off eight round slices. Place one on each salmon portion and sprinkle with a little sea salt and freshly ground black pepper. Bring the edges of the baking paper to the top, and secure with twine.

Bake for 12 minutes, or until the salmon is cooked to your liking. Serve the salmon in the parcels, for diners to unwrap at the table.

Recipe photograph on page 192

baked salmon parcels
with a herb & lemon
zest butter

◇◇◇◇◇◇◇◇◇

recipe page 191

fish & lentil stew

I have made this super simple, super speedy dish for dinner on countless occasions, yet it still surprises me how wonderful and robust it is — a stew with plenty of depth and character. It's delicious with a chunk of crusty sourdough bread.

SERVES 5–6 ◆ GF, DF (if no ghee or butter used)

2 tablespoons ghee, butter
   or olive oil
2 tablespoons rice flour, cornflour
   (cornstarch) or tapioca flour
60 g (2¼ oz/¼ cup) tomato paste
   (concentrated purée)
1 litre (35 fl oz/4 cups) good-quality
   vegetable stock
2 x 400 g (14 oz) tins lentils,
   rinsed and drained, or 3 cups
   cooked lentils
800 g (1 lb 12 oz) white fish, skin
   and any small bones removed,
   cut into bite-sized chunks
a large handful of flat-leaf (Italian)
   parsley leaves, finely chopped,
   plus extra to garnish

Melt the ghee in a large heavy-based casserole dish or saucepan over medium heat. Add the flour and tomato paste and stir for 20–30 seconds.

Add the stock and lentils, then bring to a soft boil. Add the fish and simmer over low heat for 2 minutes, or until the fish is just cooked, but not falling apart.

Remove from the heat and stir in the parsley. Season to taste with sea salt and freshly ground black pepper. Ladle into bowls, garnish with extra parsley and serve.

rosemary lamb ragù with golden sweet potato mash

A wonderfully fragrant ragù, inspired by the Sicilian combination of rich lamb, dried mint and chilli flakes. This melt-in-your-mouth dish has a deep and complex layer of flavours, making it an absolute pleasure to eat.

SERVES 4 ◆ GF

60 ml (2 fl oz/¼ cup) olive oil
6 French shallots, thinly sliced
6 garlic cloves, thinly sliced
2 teaspoons dried mint
1 teaspoon dried oregano
1 teaspoon dried rosemary
½ teaspoon chilli flakes
500 g (1 lb 2 oz) minced
    (ground) lamb
1 glass of red wine
400 g (14 oz) tin chopped
    tomatoes
2 tablespoons tomato paste
    (concentrated purée)
2 teaspoons worcestershire sauce

For the mash
1.25 kg (2 lb 12 oz) sweet potatoes,
    peeled and cut into cubes
3 tablespoons butter or olive oil
2 handfuls of grated parmesan
    cheese

To serve
grated parmesan cheese,
    for sprinkling
flat-leaf (Italian) parsley, to garnish

Heat the olive oil in a large heavy-based saucepan over medium heat. Add the shallot, garlic, dried herbs and chilli flakes. Cook, stirring, for about 5 minutes, or until the mixture smells fragrant and the shallot is slightly softened.

Add the lamb and continue to cook until browned, stirring often, and breaking up any lumps with a wooden spoon.

Stir in the wine, then leave to simmer for a few minutes, until it has evaporated. Add the tomatoes, tomato paste and worcestershire sauce. Add 250 ml (9 fl oz/1 cup) water and a good pinch of sea salt and freshly ground black pepper. Stir well, partially cover with a lid, then leave to simmer for 25 minutes.

Meanwhile, make the mash. Put the sweet potato in a saucepan and cover with water. Add a pinch of salt and bring to the boil, then reduce the heat and simmer for 15–20 minutes, or until tender. Drain well, then add the butter, parmesan and a good pinch of salt and pepper. Mash well.

Divide the mash among serving bowls, then top with the lamb ragù. Sprinkle with a little extra parmesan and parsley and serve.

quinoa pilaff with peas,
mint & parmesan

*Magically combining light, delicate flavours, this tasty pilaff is full of
grassy-green freshness. Quinoa has a spectacular fluffy texture, with a slight
crunch, and is a really good choice for vegetarians as it is high in protein. Give it
a go! I am sure you will not be disappointed. I like to serve the pilaff with a fried
egg for a balanced meal; if you're vegan, try sprinkling the pilaff with toasted seeds
for added nourishment. The pilaff is also nice cold, as a picnic or lunch dish.*

SERVES 4–6 AS A SIDE, OR 2–3 AS A LIGHT MEAL ◆ GF, DF (using olive oil),
VEG (using vegetable stock), V (using olive oil, vegetable stock and no egg)

400 g (14 oz/2 cups) quinoa,
   rinsed well
4 garlic cloves, finely chopped
500 ml (17 fl oz/2 cups)
   good-quality chicken or
   vegetable stock
2 tablespoons butter or olive oil
2 handfuls of flat-leaf (Italian)
   parsley, roughly chopped
juice of 1 lemon
fried eggs, to serve (optional)

Add the quinoa and garlic to a large saucepan. Pour in the stock and
500 ml (17 fl oz/2 cups) water. Add a pinch of sea salt and freshly ground
black pepper.

Bring to the boil, then turn the heat down low. Simmer for 20 minutes,
or until all the liquid has been absorbed.

Stir in the butter, parsley and lemon juice, mixing well. Taste, then adjust
the seasonings if you need to. Serve warm, topping each serve with a
fried egg if desired.

delightfully creamy sweet potato & apple soup with rosemary

*This fragrant, velvety soup is very nourishing and good for the soul.
Roasting the apples along with the sweet potato before blending the soup
really releases a world of gorgeous flavours.*

SERVES 4–6 ◆ GF, DF, VEG (using vegetable stock), V (using vegetable stock)

8 orange sweet potatoes, peeled
  and cut into chunks
1 garlic bulb, each clove peeled
  and lightly smashed
2 apples, sliced in half, cores
  removed
a large handful of fresh rosemary
  sprigs, plus extra to garnish
olive oil, for drizzling
1 litre (35 fl oz/4 cups) good-quality
  vegetable or chicken stock

Preheat the oven to 180°C (350°F).

Arrange the sweet potato, garlic and apple halves on a large baking tray.
Top with the rosemary, then drizzle generously with olive oil.

Roast for 30–40 minutes, or until the sweet potato and garlic are golden
and slightly caramelised.

Transfer the mixture to a blender or food processor, including the rosemary.

Heat the stock until it is hot, but not quite simmering. Carefully add half
the stock to the blender and whiz until smooth. Add the remaining stock,
one ladleful at a time, blending until the preferred consistency is achieved.
Season to taste with sea salt and freshly ground black pepper.

Gently reheat the soup, then ladle into bowls. Drizzle with a little extra
olive oil, garnish with a rosemary sprig, add another sprinkling of black
pepper and serve.

crispy almond-coated chicken roasted with artichokes & lemon

My favourite recipe in this entire book. I cannot even begin to explain how tasty this dish is, each mouthful a marvellous burst of the Mediterranean — gorgeously crispy almond-coated chicken with meltingly tender artichokes, and a hint of lemon to cut through the richness. This is serious melt-in-your-mouth goodness with a sensational sticky, sweet and salty sauce. Do give this one a go — I promise you will not be disappointed. Serve with steamed green beans or peas.

SERVES 4 ◆ GF, DF

50 g (1¾ oz/½ cup) almond meal
8 free-range chicken drumsticks
440 g (15/2 oz/1½ cups) marinated artichokes, drained and roughly chopped
a large handful of fresh oregano leaves
a large handful of pepitas (pumpkin seeds)
extra virgin olive oil, for drizzling
lemon wedges, to serve

Preheat the oven to 180°C (350°F).

Place the almond meal in a shallow bowl. Roll the chicken drumsticks in the almond meal until coated all over.

Arrange the chicken in a large baking dish, along with the artichoke. Sprinkle with the oregano, pepitas and a generous pinch of sea salt and freshly ground black pepper. Drizzle generously with olive oil.

Roast for 1 hour, or until the coating is crispy and golden and the chicken is cooked through. Serve with lemon wedges.

chocolate
pudding cakes
◇◇◇◇◇◇◇◇◇
recipe page 208

AFTER
DINNER
DELIGHTS

real proper
custard

◇◇◇◇◇◇◇◇◇

recipe page 227

Desserts are enjoyed often in our household.
Whatever the mood or season may be, a beautiful
home-made dessert is always worth the effort.

We all love a little treat every now and then, but I believe
it is important to find the balance between enjoying
sweetness in life, without going overboard.

For this reason, I prefer to use unrefined sweeteners
in my desserts, such as honey, rapadura sugar, dates, pure
maple syrup and fruit. Not only are they far more nourishing
than refined sugars or artificial sweeteners, they also add
a delicious wealth of flavour.

In this chapter you will find a gorgeous assortment of well-loved
delights, including the most wonderful spiced strawberry linzer
torte, home-made bite-sized peppermint chocolates, and the
most ridiculously simple mango and banana soft serve, which
my kids absolutely adore on a hot summer's evening.

chocolate cherry pudding cakes

Chocolate and cherry have a natural affinity for each other, and are the perfect combination in these stunningly rich and decadent delights. If you can't get hold of fresh cherries, raspberries are a luscious substitute. For a gooey and delectable centre, my secret is to ever so slightly undercook these pudding cakes. Please use good-quality dark chocolate; it really shines in this recipe and makes all the difference.

MAKES 10 ◆ GF, DF (using coconut oil), VEG

300 g (10½ oz) good-quality
  dark chocolate, melted
250 g (9 oz/1 cup) unsalted butter
  or coconut oil
150 g (5½ oz/1 cup) coconut or
  muscovado sugar
50 g (1¾ oz/½ cup) almond meal
160 g (5½ oz/1 cup) pitted
  medjool dates or dried figs,
  or 180 g (6 oz/1 cup)
  pitted prunes
6 free-range eggs
a pinch of sea salt
10 fresh cherries
icing (confectioners' sugar),
  for dusting (optional)

Preheat the oven to 180°C (350°F). Line 10 holes of a standard muffin tin with paper cases.

Add the chocolate, butter, sugar, almond meal and dates to a food processor. Add the eggs and salt and blend until smooth.

Divide the batter among the muffin holes, then place a cherry on top of each cake.

Bake for 18 minutes, or until they are still a little squishy in the centre; they will continue to cook ever so slightly as they are cooling. Remove from the oven and leave to cool in the tin. Serve dusted with icing sugar if desired.

The cakes will keep in an airtight container in a cool dark place for up to 3 days, and can be frozen for up to 2 months.

spiced strawberry linzer torte

A wholesome take on the classic Austrian torte, this delightful dessert has a wonderfully delicate and buttery almond-based pastry, and is spiced with a little cinnamon and a hint of vanilla. Traditionally, the torte is filled with jam. I have used fresh strawberries sprinkled with rapadura sugar and lemon zest for a lighter fruity touch.

SERVES 8 ◆ GF (using buckwheat or rice flour), VEG

For the pastry
125 g (4½ oz) butter, chilled
    and cubed
175 g (6 oz/1¾ cups) almond meal
230 g (8 oz/1¾ cups) buckwheat
    flour, 175 g (6 oz/1¾ cups)
    spelt flour, or 300 g (10½ oz/
    1¾ cups) rice flour, plus extra
    for dusting
100 g (3½ oz/⅔ cup) rapadura,
    coconut or muscovado sugar
1 teaspoon pure vanilla extract
1 teaspoon ground cinnamon
1 teaspoon bicarbonate of soda
    (baking soda)
2 free-range eggs

For the filling
450 g (1 lb/3 cups) strawberries,
    green hulls removed, sliced
    in half
75 g (2½ oz/½ cup) rapadura,
    coconut or muscovado sugar
juice of ½ lemon

For the topping
1 free-range egg, beaten
2 tablespoons poppy seeds

Preheat the oven to 170°C (325°F). Grease a 22 cm (8½ inch) pie tin.

To make the pastry, place all the ingredients, except the eggs, in a food processor. Pulse until the mixture resembles coarse breadcrumbs. With the motor running on low, add the eggs one at a time, and process until the mixture starts to come together like a dough.

Turn the dough out onto a floured bench, then knead for 2–3 minutes, until lovely and smooth.

Using a rolling pin, roll the dough out to about 5 mm (¼ inch) thick, then dust with extra flour. Loosely roll the pastry around the rolling pin, then carefully unroll it over the pie dish. Press the pastry into the dish and trim the edges using a sharp knife.

Combine the filling ingredients in a mixing bowl. Toss well to combine, then spoon the mixture into the pie dish.

Roll out the pastry trimmings, then slice into long strips, about 3 cm (1¼ inches) wide. Arrange the pastry strips over the strawberry filling, in a lattice pattern. Trim any excess pastry from the edges.

Gently brush the pastry with the beaten egg, then sprinkle with the poppy seeds. Bake for 35–40 minutes, or until the pastry is golden and the filling is bubbling.

Remove from the oven and leave to cool in the tin before serving. The torte will keep in an airtight container in a cool, dark place for up to 3 days.

a gorgeous apple pie
with spelt flour pastry

This is the apple pie my dreams are made of. Everyone should know how to make this blissful pie — an old faithful that's as comforting as a hot water bottle on a cold winter's night. The crust is my go-to pastry recipe — super easy to work with, always forgiving and irresistibly flaky. Serve warm, with ice cream or whipped cream if desired.

SERVES 8 ◆ VEG

For the pastry
250 g (9 oz/2½ cups) spelt flour
  (see note), plus a little extra
  for kneading
50 g (1¾ oz/⅓ cup) coconut or
  rapadura sugar
a pinch of sea salt
180 g (6 oz) butter, chilled
  and diced
2 free-range eggs

For the filling
1.5 kg (3 lb 5 oz) cooking apples,
  peeled and very thinly sliced
  (a mandoline works well for this)
60 g (2¼ oz/¼ cup) butter or
  coconut oil
115 g (4 oz/⅓ cup) honey
1 teaspoon ground cinnamon
juice of 1 lemon

To make the pastry, add the flour, sugar and sea salt to a food processor and pulse to combine. Add the butter and pulse again, until the mixture resembles fine breadcrumbs. Add the eggs and 2 tablespoons water, then process until the mixture starts to form a dough.

Turn the dough out onto a floured surface. Knead very softly for about 10–20 seconds. Shape into a ball, then wrap in plastic wrap and chill in the fridge for 25 minutes.

Preheat the oven to 180°C (350°F). Line a baking tray with baking paper.

Turn the pastry out onto a floured surface and knead for 1–2 minutes, until lovely and smooth. Using a rolling pin, roll the dough out to about 5 mm (¼ inch) thick, then dust with extra flour.

Loosely roll the pastry around the rolling pin, then carefully unroll it over the pie dish. Press the pastry into the dish and trim the edges using a sharp knife.

Combine the filling ingredients in a mixing bowl, tossing until well combined. Pile the filling into the pie dish, then gently pat down.

Bake for 45–50 minutes, or until the pastry is golden and the apple tender. Remove from the oven and allow to cool for a few minutes before serving.

note ◇◇◇◇◇◇◇◇◇◇◇◇◇◇◇◇◇◇◇◇◇◇◇◇◇◇◇◇◇◇◇◇◇◇◇◇◇

Instead of spelt flour, you could use 325 g (11½ oz/2½ cups) buckwheat flour, 300 g (10½ oz/2 cups) quinoa flour or 400 g (14 oz/2½ cups) brown rice flour for a gluten-free version.

warm coconut rice pudding with pineapple

Gorgeously creamy rice pudding is loved by just about everyone, and can be enjoyed as a comforting warm breakfast or dessert. This lovely, simple version is made using full-cream (whole) milk and flavoured with real vanilla, then topped with fresh pineapple and honey. I like it chilled in the summertime, although it is equally delicious warm.

SERVES 5–6 ◆ GF, DF (using nut or coconut milk), VEG

200 g (7 oz) arborio rice
1.25 litres (44 fl oz/5 cups)
    full-cream (whole) organic milk;
    you can also use nut or coconut
    milk for a dairy-free pudding
2 teaspoons vanilla bean paste

For the topping
160 g (5½ oz/1 cup) diced fresh
    pineapple
25 g (1 oz/¼ cup) desiccated
    coconut
honey, for drizzling

Place the rice, milk and vanilla paste in a large heavy-based saucepan. Pour in 250 ml (9 fl oz/1 cup) water, stir well, then bring to a soft boil over medium heat.

Reduce the heat to low and simmer for 30 minutes, stirring every so often, until the mixture is thick and creamy. You may need to add a little more milk towards the end.

Divide the warm rice pudding among serving bowls. Serve topped with the pineapple, coconut and a drizzle of honey.

raw tropical lime, avocado
& banana slice

*This luscious slice is made with all-natural ingredients and is packed with
healthy fats from the nuts, coconut and avocado. The filling is sensationally
creamy and rich, without being over-the-top sweet. I use raw honey in this recipe,
as I adore honey and lime as a combination, although brown rice syrup or
pure maple syrup work wonderfully also.*

MAKES 9 SLICES ◆ GF, DF, VEG, V (if no honey used)

For the crumb base
60 g (2½ oz/½ cup) sunflower
  seeds
80 g (2¾ oz/½ cup) almonds,
  or other nuts of your choice,
  roughly chopped
60 ml (2 fl oz/¼ cup) melted
  coconut oil
160 g (5½ oz/1 cup) pitted
  medjool dates
a pinch of sea salt

For the filling
grated zest and flesh of 2 limes
125 ml (4 fl oz/½ cup) melted
  coconut oil
40 g (1½ oz/¼ cup) blanched
  almonds or cashews
90 g (3¼ oz/¼ cup) honey, or
  60 ml (2 fl oz/¼ cup) maple
  syrup or brown rice syrup
flesh of 2 avocados
2 ripe bananas, peeled and
  roughly chopped

For the topping
a handful of shredded coconut

Find a slab tin measuring about 24 x 20 cm (9½ x 8 inches) and line
it with baking paper.

Add all the crumb base ingredients to a food processor. Blend until the
mixture resembles coarse breadcrumbs, then press the mixture evenly
into the tin, to a thickness of about 1 cm (½ inch).

Place all the filling ingredients in a blender or clean food processor. Blend
until smooth, then pour the mixture over the crumb base. Spread it out
evenly, using the back of a spoon. Sprinkle the shredded coconut evenly
over the top.

Place the slice in the freezer for at least 2 hours to set. Cut into squares
for serving.

The slice will keep for up to 3 days in the fridge in an airtight container,
and can be frozen for up to 2 weeks; after this time, the avocado in the
slice will start to go brown.

blackcurrant clafoutis with cinnamon cream

Clafoutis is a traditional French baked dessert, usually made with cherries, almond meal, milk and eggs. In this version I have used blackcurrants, as I love their subtle tart flavour. Delicately light in texture, this is a lovely and nurturing dessert. Serve with plain yoghurt or cream if desired.

SERVES 4 ◆ GF, DF (using nut milk), VEG

For the clafoutis

3 free-range eggs

310 ml (10¾ fl oz/1¼ cups) almond milk, or other milk of your choice

50 g (1¾ oz/½ cup) almond meal

75 g (2½ oz/½ cup) rapadura or coconut sugar

45 g (1½ oz/¼ cup) rice flour

1 tablespoon pure vanilla extract

zest of 1 lemon

a pinch of sea salt

For the topping

15 g (½ oz/¼ cup) coconut flakes

75 g (2½ oz/½ cup) fresh or frozen blackcurrants

2 tablespoons coconut flour (optional)

Preheat the oven to 180°C (350°F). Grease a 22 cm (8½ inch) baking dish or ovenproof cast-iron frying pan with coconut oil.

Add all the clafoutis ingredients to a food processor. Process until smooth, then pour into the baking dish. Top with the coconut flakes and blackcurrants.

Bake for 45 minutes, or until a skewer inserted in the middle of the clafoutis comes out clean. Remove from the oven and leave to cool slightly, then garnish with a sprinkling of coconut flour, if using.

The clafoutis is best served warm.

bella's vanilla bean ice cream

My daughter Bella and I love poking around op shops (thrift stores). It is something we quite often do together in the afternoons after school, with me searching for vintage kitchen treasures and cookbooks, and Bella finding new books and toys. One day, we came across an ice-cream machine, and were thrilled to be able to make our own wholesome ice cream from scratch. This recipe calls for full-cream (whole) organic milk, although it can be made with coconut or nut milk if you prefer. An ice-cream machine will give you much better results than trying to churn the mixture by hand.

MAKES JUST UNDER 1 LITRE (4 CUPS) ◆ GF, VEG

300 ml (10½ fl oz) thin (pouring/
   whipping) cream
300 ml (10½ fl oz) full-cream
(whole) organic milk, or other milk
   of your choice
1 vanilla bean
5 free-range egg yolks
90 g (3¼ oz/¼ cup) honey
a pinch of sea salt

Pour the cream and milk into a saucepan. Slice the vanilla bean down its length using a small sharp knife, then scoop out the tiny black seeds and add them to the milk mixture.

Warm the milk over low heat, stirring occasionally, until almost boiling — you'll see a few bubbles at the edge. Remove from the heat and set aside for 30 minutes, so that the vanilla seeds can infuse the milk.

In a heatproof bowl, lightly whisk together the egg yolks, honey and salt.

Gradually pour the milk over the egg mixture, whisking continuously until combined.

Pour the entire mixture back into the saucepan, return to a low heat and cook for 10–12 minutes, stirring continuously with a wooden spoon, until the mixture has thickened slightly. Make sure it doesn't boil, or you will end up with scrambled eggs!

Set aside to cool, then transfer to the fridge to cool completely.

Carefully pour the cooled custard into an ice-cream machine. Churn following the manufacturer's instructions until frozen, then transfer to a container. Cover and freeze until solid; this usually takes at least 4 hours.

Remove from the freezer 15 minutes before serving, to allow the ice cream to become soft enough to scoop.

The ice cream will keep in the freezer for 3 months.

mango & banana soft serve

We get pretty excited about this gloriously indulgent soft serve. It is extremely simple to prepare as it contains only two magical ingredients. Let the kids help with this one — they'll love working the food processor, and it's an impossible recipe to mess up.

SERVES 4 ♦ GF, DF, VEG, V

6 bananas, the riper the better
630 g (1 lb 6 oz/2 cups) chopped
   mango flesh

Line a baking tray with baking paper.

Peel the bananas, then cut into thick chunks. Lay the banana chunks on the baking tray, along with the mango. Place in the freezer until completely frozen — overnight is best.

Remove from the freezer and leave to thaw for about 20 minutes, or until the fruit is only half frozen.

Place the banana and mango in a food processor or blender and whiz together until they reach a soft-serve consistency.

Spoon into bowls and serve immediately.

nectarine, orange
& vanilla galette
with coconut sugar

◇◇◇◇◇◇◇◇◇

recipe page 226

nectarine, orange & vanilla galette with coconut sugar

This stunning galette is just divine. I love biting into its sweet, flaky crust and tender summer stone-fruit filling. Beautifully rustic in appearance, this dessert is very easy to put together, and can be made with any seasonal fruit hanging out on your kitchen bench; you could also use preserved fruit or frozen berries if you haven't been to the grocer recently. It is wonderful served warm, with ice cream or whipped cream.

SERVES 8 ◆ VEG

250 g (9 oz/2½ cups) spelt flour (see note on page 212), plus a little extra for kneading
50 g (1¾ oz/⅓ cup) coconut or rapadura sugar
a pinch of sea salt
180 g (6 oz) butter, chilled and diced
zest and juice of 1 large lemon
2 free-range eggs

For the filling
6 nectarines, stones removed, flesh sliced into wedges
zest and juice of 1 orange
50 g (1¾ oz/⅓ cup) coconut sugar
2 teaspoons pure vanilla extract

For the topping
1 free-range egg, lightly beaten
2–3 tablespoons coconut or rapadura sugar

Add the flour, sugar and sea salt to a food processor and pulse to combine. Add the butter and lemon zest and pulse again, until the mixture resembles fine breadcrumbs. Add the lemon juice, eggs and 2 tablespoons water, then process until the mixture starts to form a dough.

Turn the dough out onto a floured surface and knead very softly for 10–20 seconds. Shape into a ball, then wrap in plastic wrap and chill in the fridge for 25 minutes.

Preheat the oven to 180°C (350°F). Line a baking tray with baking paper.

Turn the pastry out onto a floured surface. Knead for 1–2 minutes, until lovely and smooth. Using a rolling pin, roll out the pastry on a floured surface, into a large, rustic circle about 5 mm (¼ inch) thick. Loosely roll the pastry around the rolling pin, then carefully unroll it over the baking tray.

In a large mixing bowl, gently toss the filling ingredients together until well combined.

Arrange the filling around the centre of the pastry circle. Working quickly, fold the edges of the galette over the filling, leaving some of the filling exposed. Don't worry about being too neat — rustic looks lovely! Brush the pastry with the beaten egg, then sprinkle with the sugar.

Bake for 25–30 minutes, or until the pastry is golden. Remove from the oven and allow to cool for a few minutes. Serve warm.

Recipe photograph on page 224

real proper custard

In our household, this gorgeous custard is often enjoyed for breakfast and afternoon tea, as well as dessert. It is beautifully rich from the egg yolks, and lightly sweetened with honey. Full of nourishment, this home-made version will always taste far more delicious than the processed powdered variety.

SERVES 4 ◆ GF, VEG

4 free-range egg yolks
90 g (3¼ oz/¼ cup) honey
2 teaspoons cornflour (cornstarch),
   potato starch or tapioca flour
600 ml (21 fl oz) full-cream (whole)
   organic milk (see note)
½ teaspoon pure vanilla extract

In a mixing bowl, whisk together the egg yolks, honey and cornflour until well combined.

Combine the milk and vanilla in a saucepan over medium–low heat. Bring almost to the boil, then reduce the heat to low. Carefully pour in the egg mixture, whisking all the time with a balloon whisk.

Continue to whisk over low heat for about 5 minutes, or until thickened.

Serve warm, or cover and refrigerate for up to 2 days.

note

You can also use coconut or nut milk for a dairy-free custard.

Recipe photograph on page 206

no-bake almond tarts with vanilla yoghurt mascarpone

These delightful little tarts require no baking and are wonderfully simple to prepare. The filling is a marriage of plain yoghurt, mascarpone and vanilla: perfectly creamy, yet slightly tangy. You could top these tarts with almost any type of fresh fruit. I love to use fresh berries, kiwi fruit or feijoa.

MAKES 12 ◆ GF, VEG

For the almond tart shells

200 g (7 oz/2 cups) almond meal, or other ground nuts of your choice

125 g (4½ oz/½ cup) coconut oil, chilled

2 tablespoons honey or maple syrup

a pinch of sea salt

For the filling

185 g (6½ oz/¾ cup) plain yoghurt

185 g (6½ oz/¾ cup) mascarpone cheese

1 tablespoon honey or maple syrup

1 teaspoon pure vanilla extract

For the topping

thinly sliced fresh fruit of your choice

15 g (½ oz/¼ cup) flaked or shredded coconut (optional)

Grease a standard 12-hole muffin tin with coconut oil or line with paper cases. (I like to use silicon muffin moulds, as I find the tarts easier to remove.)

Put the tart shell ingredients in a food processor and blend until well combined. Press evenly into the muffin holes, then place in the fridge or freezer for at least 2 hours to set.

Combine the filling ingredients in a bowl, mixing well. Divide the filling evenly among the tart cases. Top with the fruit slices, then sprinkle with the coconut if desired.

These tarts will keep in an airtight container for up to 2 days; I find they are best kept in the fridge.

vegan dandelion torte with a dark chocolate ganache

Here is my recipe for an irresistibly rich and fudgy vegan torte,
made entirely of wholesome ingredients. The subtle bitterness of the dandelion
root somehow makes the cocoa in this torte taste more chocolatey and rich. I have
used rapadura sugar as a light sweetener; if you haven't tried it before, I would
strongly recommend it. This lovely mellow-tasting sugar has not been heated,
contains more nutrients than most other types of sugar, and is metabolised
more slowly by the body than most other sweeteners.

SERVES 8 ◆ GF, DF, VEG, V

For the torte
150 g (5½ oz/1½ cups) almond meal
375 ml (13 fl oz/1½ cups) coconut
　cream
2 tablespoons ground dandelion
　root (or ground coffee)
90 g (3¼ oz/½ cup) linseeds
　(flaxseeds)
75 g (2½ oz/½ cup) rapadura,
　muscovado or coconut sugar
75 g (2½ oz/½ cup) chopped dark
　chocolate, melted
1 teaspoon bicarbonate of soda
　(baking soda)

For the topping
75 g (2½ oz/½ cup) chopped dark
　chocolate (preferably one
　containing at least 80% cocoa)
60 ml (2 fl oz/¼ cup) coconut
　cream
shaved dark chocolate, for
　sprinkling

Preheat the oven to 160°C (315°F). Grease a 22 cm (8½ inch) cake tin with coconut oil.

Add all the torte ingredients to a food processor and blend until smooth. Spoon the batter into the cake tin, smoothing the surface evenly.

Bake for 35 minutes, or until a skewer inserted into the middle of the cake comes out clean. The outside edges should be slightly crispy, and the inside slightly soft to touch.

Remove from the oven and leave to cool completely in the tin, before carefully transferring the torte to a plate.

To make the topping, combine the chocolate and coconut cream in a small saucepan over very low heat. Stir gently until completely melted into a silky-smooth sauce. Remove from the heat and leave to cool slightly.

Pour the chocolate sauce carefully onto the centre of the torte, then smooth it out evenly with the back of a spoon, leaving a 2 cm (¾ inch) gap from the edge of the torte.

Leave the topping to set for at least 30 minutes. Sprinkle with shaved chocolate just before slicing and serving.

The torte will keep in an airtight container for 2–3 days; it is best kept at room temperature, as it goes quite hard in the fridge.

poached pears with chocolate sauce & vanilla cream

I once whipped up this dessert when we had unexpected guests pop in for dinner. It took all of five minutes to prepare, and tasted heavenly. This simple recipe uses tinned or preserved pears, paired with rich, bittersweet dark chocolate and the unexpected surprise of a little ginger. You could also use about six fresh pears if you have them; slice them into wedges and cook them in a frying pan in a little coconut oil before serving, to give them a nice colour and soften them up.

SERVES 6 ◆ GF, VEG

2 x 400 g (14 oz) tins pears in
    unsweetened juice, or preserved
    pears; reserve the juice
1 teaspoon ground ginger
1 teaspoon ground cinnamon
1 tablespoon honey, maple syrup
    or brown rice syrup
250 g (9 oz) block of dark
    chocolate, at least 80% cocoa
    if possible, broken into pieces
300 ml (10½ fl oz) whipping cream
1 teaspoon pure vanilla extract
35 g (1¼ oz/¼ cup) toasted
    hazelnuts, crushed

Put the pears in a mixing bowl, along with a small glug of the juice that the pears were tinned or preserved in — just enough to keep the fruit moist. Reserve the rest of the juice for the chocolate sauce.

To the pears, add the ginger, cinnamon and honey, then toss to combine.

Add the chocolate to a small saucepan. Pour in 250 ml (9 fl oz/1 cup) of the reserved pear juice. Heat slowly over low heat, stirring until the chocolate has melted and you have a lovely, velvety, luxurious sauce. Remove from the heat and set aside to cool slightly.

Put the cream and vanilla in a large bowl. Beat with an egg-beater until thick and creamy, being careful not to overwhip.

Divide the pears among serving bowls. Top with a dollop of the cream. Add a good drizzle of the chocolate sauce, then sprinkle with the hazelnuts. This dessert is best served immediately.

raw fig tart with milk chocolate ganache & almond date crust

Naturally full of gluten-free goodness, this tart is perfectly sweet and wonderfully simple to prepare. I've used mascarpone cheese for the filling, but have also included a dairy-free version made with cashew nuts. If figs aren't your thing, you can use pretty much any type of fresh fruit. You can also replace the almond meal in the crust with other ground nuts of your choice. Enjoy.

SERVES 8 ◆ GF, DF (using coconut oil and cashew ganache),
VEG, V (using coconut oil, cashew ganache and no honey)

150 g (5½ oz/1½ cups) almond meal

90 g (3¼ oz/1 cup) desiccated coconut

160 g (5½ oz/1 cup) pitted medjool dates

80 ml (2½ fl oz/⅓ cup) melted coconut oil or butter

4–6 fresh figs, thinly sliced

For the mascarpone ganache

220 g (7¾ oz/1 cup) mascarpone cheese

2 tablespoons good-quality unsweetened cocoa powder

2 tablespoons honey, maple syrup or brown rice syrup

For the cashew ganache

155 g (5½ oz/1 cup) cashews, soaked in water overnight, then drained well

2 tablespoons melted coconut oil

2 tablespoons good-quality unsweetened cocoa powder

2 tablespoons honey, maple syrup or brown rice syrup

Grease a 22 cm (8½ inch) cake tin with coconut oil or butter. Line the base and sides with baking paper.

Place the almond meal, coconut and dates in a food processor. Pour in the melted coconut oil and add a pinch of sea salt. Blend for 1–2 minutes, or until the mixture starts to come together like a dough.

Press the mixture evenly into the cake tin, pressing the edges up slightly around the side of the tin.

Add the ganache ingredients to a food processor and blitz until smooth. Taste, then add a little more sweetener if you prefer (I don't like the ganache too sweet).

Carefully spoon the ganache over the crust, spreading it out evenly with the back of a spoon. Arrange the fig slices around the top, then place in the fridge for at least 2 hours to set.

Serve chilled. The tart will keep in an airtight container in the fridge for up to 2 days.

peppermint dark chocolates

The best things in life are simple — or at least the best recipes are.
These home-made chocolates are a cinch to prepare, and contain only
a few natural ingredients. I love to keep a container of these chocolates
in the freezer for a small indulgent after-dinner treat. This recipe
makes around 15 bite-sized pieces, but you can easily halve
it to make a smaller quantity.

MAKES ABOUT 15 ◆ GF, DF, VEG, V (if no honey used)

175 g (6 oz/½ cup) honey, or
125 ml (4 fl oz/½ cup) maple
syrup or brown rice syrup
250 g (9 oz/1 cup) coconut oil
or cocoa butter
125 g (4½ oz/½ cup) nut butter;
I use almond, but peanut or
cashew work well also
60 g (2¼ oz/½ cup) good-quality
unsweetened cocoa powder
2 teaspoons pure peppermint
extract
a pinch of sea salt (optional)
edible flowers, to garnish (optional)

In a small saucepan over very low heat, gently melt the honey, coconut oil and nut butter together. Stir in the cocoa, peppermint extract and sea salt, if using. Whisk until smooth.

Carefully pour the chocolate mixture into small paper cases or chocolate moulds; if possible, choose ones that are about 2 cm (¾ inch) in diameter. Place in the freezer for 1–2 hours, or until set.

These chocolates are best kept in an airtight container in the fridge, or in the freezer. They will keep in the fridge for up to 1 week, and in the freezer for up to 1 month.

To serve, simply remove from the freezer and pop the chocolates out of their moulds. Garnish with edible flowers if desired.

prune & earl grey sponge pudding with a hint of ginger

Here's a scrumptious dessert that offers pure happiness with every mouthful. The prunes and dates are simmered in earl grey tea for a gorgeous infusion, then folded into a sweet almond batter and baked in the oven. The pudding is then topped with a fantastic caramel sauce made with coconut cream and honey. Perfectly sweet and decadent — fabulous for impressing dinner guests.

SERVES 8 ◆ GF, DF (using coconut oil), VEG

For the pudding

2 earl grey tea bags

110 g (3¾ oz/½ cup) pitted prunes

80 g (2¾ oz/½ cup) pitted
　medjool dates

3 free-range eggs

60 g (2¼ oz/¼ cup) coconut oil
　or butter

250 g (9 oz/1 cup) almond butter,
　or other nut butter of your choice

2 tablespoons honey, maple syrup
　or brown rice syrup

1 teaspoon bicarbonate of soda
　(baking soda)

1 teaspoon apple cider vinegar

For the coconut caramel sauce

400 ml (14 fl oz) full-fat coconut
　cream

175 g (6 oz/½ cup) honey

To make the pudding, combine the tea bags, prunes and dates in a small saucepan. Cover with about 250 ml (9 fl oz/1 cup) water and bring to a soft boil. Simmer for 10–15 minutes, or until all the water has cooked off, and the fruit is soft and pulpy. Remove from the heat. Discard the tea bags and set the prune mixture aside to cool.

Meanwhile, preheat the oven to 160°C (315°F). Grease a 26 cm (10½ inch) cake tin with coconut oil; for this recipe I've used a ring (bundt) tin.

Place the cooled prunes and dates in a food processor. Add the remaining pudding ingredients and blend for a minute or so, until the batter is smooth and creamy.

Spoon the batter into the cake tin. Bake for 25–30 minutes, or until a skewer inserted into the middle of the pudding comes out clean.

While the pudding is baking, prepare the coconut caramel sauce. Combine the coconut cream and honey in a saucepan and bring to a soft boil over medium heat. Turn the heat down to low and simmer for 20–25 minutes, or until the caramel becomes a lovely golden colour. Stir often towards the end, as the caramel can burn easily.

Serve the pudding warm, with a drizzle of the coconut caramel sauce.

white chocolate coconut roughs

Simple and wonderfully delicious, these extraordinary little white chocolate bites are made using only four beautiful ingredients. The quality of the cocoa butter is essential here — only the good stuff will give you the true white-chocolate essence. I sometimes also add a little unsweetened cocoa powder to the mixture, which works an absolute treat if you'd like more of a milk-chocolate effect.

MAKES 8 ◆ GF, DF, VEG

125 g (4½ oz/½ cup) cocoa butter
115 g (4 oz/⅓ cup) honey
1 teaspoon vanilla bean paste
60 g (2¼ oz/1 cup) shredded
  coconut

Line eight holes of a standard muffin tin with paper cases.

In a small saucepan, gently melt together the cocoa butter and honey over low heat.

Stir in the vanilla paste and coconut, and continue to stir for 2–3 minutes, or until the mixture becomes thick and creamy.

Divide the mixture among the muffin holes. Place in the freezer for 2–3 hours, or until set, then enjoy!

The coconut roughs are best stored in an airtight container in the fridge or freezer. They will keep in the fridge for up to 1 week, and in the freezer for up to 1 month.

almond snowballs

*Fabulously festive, these fudgy little treats contain only a small handful
of simple ingredients and take less than ten minutes to prepare. I've added
a splash of Frangelico for a wonderful hint of hazelnut, but most types
of liqueur would work well too. Alternatively you could leave it out
altogether and use lemon or orange juice instead.*

MAKES ABOUT 30 ◆ GF, DF, VEG, V

200 g (7 oz/2 cups) almond meal
125 g (4½ oz/1 cup) unrefined
  icing (confectioners') sugar,
  plus an extra 60 g (2¼ oz/½ cup)
  for dusting
80 ml (2½ fl oz/⅓ cup) melted
  coconut oil
3–4 tablespoons Frangelico or
  other hazelnut liqueur

Add the almond meal, 125 g (4½ oz/1 cup) icing sugar and coconut oil to
a food processor. Pulse until the mixture resembles coarse breadcrumbs.

With the motor running on low, gradually add the liqueur, one tablespoon
at a time, until the mixture starts to come together slightly.

Transfer to a small bowl, then use your hands to form the mixture into
small balls.

Place the extra icing sugar in a separate bowl, then roll the balls in the
icing sugar until well coated.

Transfer to a plate, then place in the fridge to set for at least 30 minutes.

The truffles can be kept in an airtight container at room temperature,
but I find they are best kept in the fridge. They will keep for 3–4 days.

salted banana & almond butter caramel mousse

With subtle hints of caramel from the almond butter, this whipped banana mousse tastes sinfully good. It is naturally sweetened with ripe bananas and a hint of honey, although you could also use pure maple syrup or brown rice syrup if you prefer. This luscious yet light and fluffy mousse is very simple to prepare; you can also freeze the mousse mixture in ice-cream moulds, for an equally delicious frozen treat.

SERVES 5–6 ◆ GF, DF, VEG, V (if no honey used)

For the mousse
3 ripe bananas, peeled and
   roughly chopped
400 ml (14 fl oz) coconut cream
2 teaspoons pure vanilla extract
125 g (4½ oz/½ cup) almond butter
125 ml (4 fl oz/½ cup) melted
   coconut oil
90 g (3¼ oz/¼ cup) honey, or
   60 ml (2 fl oz/¼ cup) maple
   syrup or brown rice syrup
a good pinch of sea salt

For the topping
2 bananas, peeled and sliced
   into rounds
ground cinnamon, for sprinkling
shredded coconut, for sprinkling

Place all the mousse ingredients in a blender or food processor. Blitz until lovely and smooth.

Carefully pour the mixture into small glass jars or ramekins that are about 375 ml (13 fl oz/1½ cups) in capacity.

Pop in the fridge to set for at least 2 hours.

Without the topping, the mouse will keep covered in the fridge for 1–2 days, or in the freezer for up to 2 weeks.

To serve, top each mousse with several slices of banana, and a sprinkling of cinnamon and coconut.

thanks

To Bella and Obi, my two gorgeous children. Thank you for helping to inspire many of the recipes in this book, for being the ultimate recipe testers; and for always being eager to help out whenever possible.

Valentin, you are my pillar in a rocky landscape. I am truly grateful for your endless support, love, patience, and for letting me spend hours on end in the kitchen.

Mum and Dad, thank you for instilling in me a love for food, right from the early days of living above the restaurant. You taught me to stand up for what I believe in and to prevail when things get a little tough. The more I grow as a mother, the more I notice all of the little things that you do.

To each and every member of my incredible family — my beautiful sister Melanie and Sean, you are always there when I need a helping hand; Grandma and Grandad, for being such an important part of our lives, and for your endless years of support; Pauline, for your generosity, love and gorgeous vintage gifts; Debbie, for letting me borrow your lovely cookbooks! Grandad Skip, Grandma Clare, I love you both and wish that I could spend more time with you.

Diana, Miro and the Ozich clan, I am so glad to be a part of your beautiful family. You have welcomed me with open arms, and for that I am truly grateful.

Beautiful Imogen. Thank you for your boundless love, guidance and friendship. You are a shining star.

To all of my close friends who inspire me every day to live what I love with great passion. I love you all.

To Hannah, I couldn't have picked a more amazing person to open a cafe with. I am so proud of what we have created together — Mondays is truly a place of inspiration, and I am so happy to have built such a strong friendship with you along the way.

To my publisher, Corinne. You have believed in me since day one. I am so grateful for your encouragement, guidance and advice over the last couple of years. Thank you for sharing this journey with me.

Madeleine, thank you for bringing your vision to the design. You have imbued the book with a simple elegance which is more beautiful than I could have imagined. A special mention also to Emma, Katri and the rest of the fantastic team at Murdoch Books. You have all been so wonderful to work with.

Thank you, Greta, for capturing the lovely images at our afternoon family gathering, and to Gem for helping to style the occasion.

And, of course, to all of you who read my blog, or have simply connected in some way or another. Your ongoing support, heartfelt comments and kindness have influenced me in a way that I am truly grateful for. Thank you for sharing this journey with me.

Eleanor x

index

about the author

As a child, Eleanor Ozich lived above her parents' restaurant in Auckland, New Zealand; she has been a self-confessed food lover ever since. She is a self-taught cook who has worked as a food stylist and photographer for various publications, including *Taste Magazine*, and is a writer for *Viva - The New Zealand Herald* and *The Healthy Food Guide*. In addition to her 45,000 Facebook and blog fans, she is establishing a loyal following at her Auckland café, Mondays Wholefoods, and is the author of *My Petite Kitchen Cookbook* (2014) for Murdoch Books.

Published in 2015 by Murdoch Books, an imprint of Allen & Unwin.

Murdoch Books Australia
83 Alexander Street
Crows Nest NSW 2065
Phone: +61 (0) 2 8425 0100
Fax: +61 (0) 2 9906 2218
www.murdochbooks.com.au
info@murdochbooks.com.au

Murdoch Books UK
Erico House, 6th Floor
93–99 Upper Richmond Road
Putney, London SW15 2TG
Phone: +44 (0) 20 8785 5995
Fax: +44 (0) 20 8785 5985
www.murdochbooks.co.uk
info@murdochbooks.co.uk

For Corporate Orders & Custom Publishing contact Noel Hammond,
National Business Development Manager, Murdoch Books Australia

Publisher: Corinne Roberts
Photographer and Stylist: Eleanor Ozich
Designer: Madeleine Kane
Editorial Manager: Emma Hutchinson
Editor: Katri Hilden
Production Manager: Mary Bjelobrk

The images on the back cover and pages 2–3, 7–8, 62, 101, 104, 107, 109, 122, 141, 209, 246,
248 and 249 were photographed by Greta Kenyon. All other images by Eleanor Ozich.

A cataloguing-in-publication entry is available from the catalogue
of the National Library of Australia at www.nla.gov.au.
A catalogue record for this book is available from the British Library.

Colour reproduction by Splitting Image, Clayton, Victoria.
Printed by Hang Tai Printing Company Limited, China.

IMPORTANT: Those who might be at risk from the effects of salmonella poisoning (the elderly,
pregnant women, young children and those suffering from immune deficiency diseases) should
consult their doctor with any concerns about eating raw eggs.
OVEN GUIDE: You may find cooking times vary depending on the oven you are using.
We have used a fan-forced oven in these recipes. As a general rule, set the temperature
for a conventional oven 20°C (35°F) higher than indicated in the recipe.
MEASURES GUIDE: We have used 20 ml (4 teaspoon) tablespoon measures. If you are using a
15 ml (3 teaspoon) tablespoon add an extra teaspoon of the ingredient for each tablespoon specified.